THE RESPONSIBLE ELECTORATE

V. O. Key, Jr., 1908 – 1963
JONATHAN TRUMBULL PROFESSOR
OF AMERICAN HISTORY AND GOVERNMENT,
HARVARD UNIVERSITY

THE RESPONSIBLE ELECTORATE

RATIONALITY IN PRESIDENTIAL VOTING
1936–1960

V. O. KEY, Jr.

WITH THE ASSISTANCE OF MILTON C. CUMMINGS, JR.

FOREWORD BY ARTHUR MAASS

THE BELKNAP PRESS OF
HARVARD UNIVERSITY PRESS

CAMBRIDGE, MASSACHUSETTS

1966

CONTENTS

FOREWORD BY
ARTHUR MAASS

The publication of this book is a happy event for those
who are optimistic about democracy. "The perverse and
unorthodox argument of this little book," says V. O. Key,
Jr., "is that voters are not fools."

Such an argument is unorthodox because some social
scientists, using data and analytical techniques similar to
Key's, have for years been teaching us something different.

From his analysis of presidential campaign data of recent decades, Key finds that the American voter and
electorate are neither "strait-jacketed by social determinants" nor "moved by subconscious urges triggered by
devilishly skillful propagandists." The portrait that
emerges is rather that of "an electorate moved by concern about central and relevant questions of public policy,
of governmental performance, and of executive personality."

When V. O. Key in April 1963 was struck by an illness

Note: Professor Maass is chairman of the Department of Government,
Harvard University.

from which he was unable to recover, he was working with intense urgency on this manuscript, in part, as his close friends have testified, because he knew that these "perverse" findings were of basic importance for both the theory and the practice of democracy in America.

Broadly, Key's method is to classify voters in presidential elections as standpatters (those who vote for the candidate of the same party in successive elections), switchers, and new voters, and to determine whether there are significant correlations between the presidential choice of these three types of voters and their opinions of the issues, events, and candidates of the campaigns.

From the data on the actions and attitudes of the shifting voters, Key concludes that they move from party to party in a manner that is broadly consistent with their policy preferences, and that switchers are far more numerous than is commonly supposed. The data on those voters who stand pat with their party from election to election do not lead to a very different conclusion, however. On the average, "the standpatters do not have to behave as mugwumps to keep their consciences clear; they are already where they ought to be in the light of their policy attitudes."

The major conclusions to be drawn from Key's findings are first, that political man is rational, and second, that the political institutions that he has developed, at least those for election of the president, are rational too.

In elaborating his argument Key shows certain characteristics that are familiar to those who have followed his work closely over the years. His deep commitment to democratic and human values and his optimism about the human race are combined with superb craftsmanship, a fine sensitivity to the relevance and irrelevance of political data and arguments, and a hardheadedness that ensures that moral purpose never passes as a cover for sloppy analysis. Thus Key is unsympathetic with, and distrustful of, political and behavioral theories that degrade the rationality of man and of the institutions that man creates freely; and with a great mastery and inventiveness of technique, he is able to prove that many such theories are false. I can illustrate this with several examples.

(1) It has been popular among political scientists and commentators to analyze election returns according to the voting behavior of large groups of persons with like attributes: occupation, religion, residence, education; and to imply that the imperatives of these economic and demographic factors guide the voting. Despite recent efforts of some political scientists to discourage this use of group imperatives, an astonishing number of people persist in doing so. Key is unsympathetic to the unflattering, deterministic implications of this analytic technique, and he shows that the technique is faulty. Gross characteristics of groups of individuals serve as an adequate indication of attitudes only when the issues of the campaign affect directly and clearly the members of the group. "The fact that a person is, say, a Negro serves as an index to what he believes and to why he votes as he does only when an election concerns Negroes as Negroes and when the members of the group are aware of the issue and see it as basic among their concerns of the moment." Where gross data indicate, for example, that 70 per cent of businessmen voted one way, Key invariably asks the question why 30 per cent did not vote their apparent economic interests; and the answer not infrequently is that the classification provided by the gross data is irrelevant. Furthermore, he finds that even where group attitudes are present, voters' individual policy preferences are important. To

understand elections, the investigator should examine directly the voters' attitudes about issues and other questions of the campaign. This is precisely what Key does in this book.

(2) Some political commentators have found a significant factor of irrationality in the way we elect the president. This they derive from the frequency of elections in which the same party retains power, and from their assumption that this is the consequence of simple repetitive voting. Key inquires, as most others have not, about the process by which a majority party maintains its dominance, and he finds that its apparently stable majority may be in fact highly changeful. The popular majority does not hold together like a ball of sticky popcorn; no sooner has it been constructed than it begins to crumble. "A series of maintaining elections occurs only in consequence of a complex process of interaction between government and populace in which old friends are sustained, old enemies are converted into new friends, old friends become even bitter opponents, and new voters are attracted to the cause." Electoral majorities, then, although they may have a stable base, are frequently majorities of the moment, *ad hoc* majorities created by the voters' responses to the actions and policies of government.

(3) Some voting studies have concluded that the stand-pat voter is on the average more interested and more intelligent than the switchers; that those who most readily change their party voting preferences are the least interested and the most inconsistent in their beliefs. Since switchers contribute the necessary flexibility to our political system, this means that the system's rationality depends on the "least admirable" voters. Confronted with this pessimistic conclusion for democratic government,

Key is impelled to a careful re-examination and reinterpretation of the evidence. First he develops a different, and for his purposes more reliable, definition of a switching voter as one who changes his party vote from one election to another, rather than one who changes his views during a campaign. He then finds that although the characteristics of the switchers can vary from election to election, they are not necessarily either less informed or less involved than the standpatters. In some elections, at least, they do not differ significantly from standpatters in their average level of education, in the frequency of their "don't know" or "no opinion" answers to public policy questions, or in their level of interest in politics. The major factors that distinguish switchers from standpatters are those of issues and opinions of presidential candidates' qualities. "Those who switch do so to support governmental policies or outlooks with which they agree, not because of subtle psychological or sociological peculiarities." Thus the political system is not held together by a buffer function of the uninterested voter.

(4) Some political writers have made much of an irrational cult of personality in presidential elections. While granting that personality plays a role in voting and that our data and analytical tools do not permit completely satisfactory appraisals of this role, Key rejects the cult of personality, with its disturbing implications about the motivation of voters and the rationality of the political system. With respect to the claim that personality cult accounts for Roosevelt's re-elections, he says poignantly that "it becomes ridiculous immediately if one contemplates what the fate of Franklin Delano Roosevelt would have been had he from 1933 to 1936 stood for those policies which were urged upon the country by the reactionaries of the day." And as for the pretended power of the father

image of Eisenhower, Key doubts the necessity of resorting to such "dubious hypotheses" to explain the response of the electorate.

(5) Key's study confirms earlier findings that the electorate judges retrospectively. Voters respond most clearly to those events that they have experienced and observed; proposals for the future, being hazy and uncertain, neither engage the voter nor govern his actions in the same degree. From this evidence some commentators conclude that voters are playing a largely irrelevant role, for their choices in a presidential election should be based on the candidates' positions on new issues and future policies and programs.

Key does not hesitate to draw attention to the limiting consequences of the evidence. He notes that the minority party cannot play the role of an imaginative advocate, for it is captive of the majority. It gains votes principally from among those who are disappointed by, or disapprove of, the Administration. "Thus, as a matter of practical politics, it must appear to be a common scold rather than a bold exponent of innovation." But Key is also quick to point out that a combination of the electorate's retrospective judgment and the custom of party accountability enables the electorate in fact to exercise a prospective influence; for governments, and parties, and candidates "must worry, not about the meaning of past elections, but about their fate at future elections." The most effective weapon of popular control in a democratic system is the capacity of the electorate to throw a party from power.

To uncover the true nature of American voting behavior and the functions that the electorate and elections perform in the system as a whole, Key wanted to study a series of presidential elections extending over a considerable period of time and including campaigns and results of considerable variety, as did those of 1936, 1948, 1952, and 1960. To do this he had to tap data sources (largely Gallup polls) that previously had been eschewed by many analysts of voting behavior, in part because the data were considered to be soft. (There were questions about the methods used to select the samples, construct and test the questions, conduct the interviews, test the reliability of a voter's recall of his vote four years earlier, etc.) To use these data, therefore, Key had to improvise techniques of analysis as well as apply tests of significance and reliability. At these tasks he was, of course, expert, but nonetheless he corresponded with several professional associates to get their reactions to what he was doing. After a careful examination of this correspondence, of Key's comments on it, of the dating of the correspondence in relation to that of successive drafts of the chapters, and above all of the text itself, Professor Cummings and I have no doubt that Key was satisfied that his data were of sufficient quality to support his analytical techniques and that the techniques were adequate to support his findings.

Key anticipated two possible objections to his attribution of significance to the parallelism of policy preferences and the direction of the vote. It might be claimed that when voters are interviewed they improvise policy views that seem to be consistent with the way they plan to vote for other reasons entirely. Key believed that although this doubtless occurs to some unknown extent, its importance should be discounted, for a voter must be fairly well informed if he is able to simulate a pattern of policy preferences that is consistent with his intended vote. A second objection might be that policy preferences are merely views that voters who are identified with a political party perceive as the orthodox party line. Key affirms that the doctrines of the party leadership can shape the policy preferences of many persons, but here too he discounts the significance of the phenomenon for his argument. Although this type of formation of policy attitudes may occur among standpatters, it is not even relevant for the millions of switching voters at each presidential election who can play a decisive role in the outcome. Finally, and with regard to both of these objections, Key points out that it is the parallelism of vote and policy that is significant, not its origin. However the opinions come into being, their supportive function in the political system should be the same.

V. O. Key died a year before the 1964 election, and before most observers thought that Barry Goldwater had a real chance to become the Republican presidential nominee. The relationships between the voters' policy preferences and their votes in 1964 are still being studied by the analysts. Yet the broad pattern of the 1964 results appears to confirm Key's thesis that voters on the average base their vote decisions on the issue positions of the candidates and on their expectations concerning how the candidates would perform as president.

Compared with 1960, and with most other presidential elections in recent years, the candidates were poles apart in 1964. The oft-noted absence of a meaningful dialogue on issues in the campaign only masked the fact that there was a wide gap between the policy positions the two candidates espoused on such vital matters as civil rights, domestic welfare legislation, and, many voters thought, on the restraint the candidate would exercise as president on questions involving war or peace.

There is evidence that many Republicans voted for Barry Goldwater despite misgivings about many of his policy positions. But Goldwater's determination to give the voters "a choice, not an echo" seems also to have wrenched an extraordinarily large number of voters from their traditional party loyalties. An election in which the State of Mississippi votes 87 per cent Republican, while, nationwide, one Republican in every five supports the Democratic presidential nominee points up the importance that policy considerations can assume when the choice given the voters on issues is sharply drawn.

PREFACE BY
MILTON C. CUMMINGS, Jr.

This study of American presidential elections was more than three-fourths completed by V. O. Key, Jr., before his death. Chapters 1 and 2 were finished and had been labeled "final drafts." Chapters 3 and 4 were in the "working draft" stage, with some marginal notes in Key's handwriting indicating possible changes or points to be amplified. Chapter 5, on the 1960 election, had been started, but not finished. There was, however, a first draft of the introduction to Chapter 5 and, perhaps even more important, a complete set of finished tables. There was also a brief outline of some of the points to be made in putting prose around the tables. For Chapter 6, the Conclusion, there was only an outline in Professor Key's handwriting.

In editing the manuscript for publication, I had several sources on which to draw in attempting to determine what

Note: In 1964, the year after V. O. Key's death, Milton C. Cummings, Jr., who had taken his Ph.D. under Professor Key in 1960, was asked to prepare Key's unfinished manuscript for publication. Cummings was then a senior staff member of the Brookings Institution. In September 1965 he became an associate professor of political science at the Johns Hopkins University.

Professor Key might have done had he been able to finish this book. These were: Key's own marginal notes, made in the draft chapters; his own handwritten outline prepared for each chapter; and his correspondence with other scholars and with the Roper Center, in which he frequently discussed how his thinking was developing. In most of the instances where I have made changes in the manuscript, one or more of these sources provided an indication of what Key was planning to do. Nevertheless, I have tried to make as few changes as possible in the material Professor Key left, and, where they appeared to be needed, to indicate clearly what was altered in the original manuscript. Thus, in Chapters 1 through 4, all substantive changes were handled in editor's notes, and only a few of these were required. Chapter 5, on the other hand, was for the most part unwritten. Yet even here Key's notes and correspondence and the introduction to the chapter gave some clues to his intentions; and there also were some marginal notes on a set of the tables which were particularly helpful. With these materials I have tried to provide an interpretation of the 1960 election that is roughly consistent with what V. O. Key might have written. I hasten to add, however, that he might have brought additional insights to the problem that eluded me, and that the responsibility for the chapter's shortcomings is mine and not his.

For the concluding Chapter 6, a decision was made to present Key's brief outline exactly as it stood, rather than to draft a full chapter based on his notes. The outline is short, and doubtless Key would have modified and expanded on it with his own inimitable sense of craftsmanship and of the subtleties and nuances of the data with which he worked. Yet from the outline the main argument of the book emerges clearly; and this outline contains some of Key's final reflections on the significance of policy considerations in the choice made by the American voter on election day.

If Key were writing this preface I am sure that he would want to express his thanks to Miss Beverly Bach, his research assistant, and to Professor Philip K. Hastings and the Roper Public Opinion Research Center, Williamstown, Massachusetts, of which he is the director, for providing access to the data on which this study is mainly based.

NOTE ON THE TABLES

The fifty-seven tables of this book show the voting behavior, or intended behavior, of various groups of people interviewed by survey organizations and classified in accordance with their policy views or other characteristics.

The tables consist largely of percentages followed by numbers in parentheses. The numbers in parentheses, technically known as N, are the numbers of poll respondents on which the percentages are based. Thus the percentage "18," followed by "(7,645)," means 18 per cent of 7,645 cases. Further clarification for the nontechnical reader will be found in the first few tables, beginning with Table 2.1 on page 14.

The tables are numbered by chapters. There are none in Chapter 1. Those in Chapter 2 are numbered 2.1 through 2.5, those in Chapter 3 are numbered 3.1 through 3.17, and so on.

ABBREVIATIONS USED IN TABLES

AIPO, meaning American Institute of Public Opinion (Gallup poll)

NORC, meaning National Opinion Research Center, University of Chicago

THE RESPONSIBLE ELECTORATE

THE VOICE OF THE PEOPLE: AN ECHO

In his reflective moments even the most experienced politician senses a nagging curiosity about why people vote as they do. His power and his position depend upon the outcome of the mysterious rites we perform as opposing candidates harangue the multitudes who finally march to the polls to prolong the rule of their champion, to thrust him, ungratefully, back into the void of private life, or to raise to eminence a new tribune of the people. What kinds of appeals enable a candidate to win the favor of the great god, The People? What circumstances move voters to shift their preferences in this direction or that? What clever propaganda tactic or slogan led to this result? What mannerism of oratory or style of rhetoric produced another outcome? What band of electors rallied to this candidate to save the day for him? What policy of state attracted the devotion of another bloc of voters? What action repelled a third sector of the electorate?

The victorious candidate may claim with assurance that he has the answers to all such questions. He may regard his success as vindication of his beliefs about why voters vote as they do. And he may regard the swing of the vote

1

to him as indubitably a response to the campaign positions he took, as an indication of the acuteness of his intuitive estimates of the mood of the people, and as a ringing manifestation of the esteem in which he is held by a discriminating public. This narcissism assumes its most repulsive form among election winners who have championed intolerance, who have stirred the passions and hatreds of people, or who have advocated causes known by decent men to be outrageous or dangerous in their long-run consequences. No functionary is more repugnant or more arrogant than the unjust man who asserts, with a color of truth, that he speaks from a pedestal of popular approbation.

It thus can be a mischievous error to assume, because a candidate wins, that a majority of the electorate shares his views on public questions, approves his past actions, or has specific expectations about his future conduct. Nor does victory establish that the candidate's campaign strategy, his image, his television style, or his fearless stand against cancer and polio turned the trick. The election returns establish only that the winner attracted a majority of the votes—assuming the existence of a modicum of rectitude in election administration. They tell us precious little about why the plurality was his.

For a glaringly obvious reason, electoral victory cannot be regarded as necessarily a popular ratification of a candidate's outlook. The voice of the people is but an echo. The output of an echo chamber bears an inevitable and invariable relation to the input. As candidates and parties clamor for attention and vie for popular support, the people's verdict can be no more than a selective reflection from among the alternatives and outlooks presented to them. Even the most discriminating popular judgment can reflect only ambiguity, uncertainty, or even foolishness if

2

those are the qualities of the input into the echo chamber. A candidate may win despite his tactics and appeals rather than because of them. If the people can choose only from among rascals, they are certain to choose a rascal.

Scholars, though they have less at stake than do politicians, also have an abiding curiosity about why voters act as they do. In the past quarter of a century they have vastly enlarged their capacity to check the hunches born of their curiosities. The invention of the sample survey—the most widely known example of which is the Gallup poll—enabled them to make fairly trustworthy estimates of the characteristics and behaviors of large human populations. This method of mass observation revolutionized the study of politics—as well as the management of political campaigns. The new technique permitted large-scale tests to check the validity of old psychological and sociological theories of human behavior. These tests led to new hunches and new theories about voting behavior, which could, in turn, be checked and which thereby contributed to the extraordinary ferment in the social sciences during recent decades.

The studies of electoral behavior by survey methods cumulate into an imposing body of knowledge which conveys a vivid impression of the variety and subtlety of factors that enter into individual voting decisions. In their first stages in the 1930's the new electoral studies chiefly lent precision and verification to the working maxims of practicing politicians and to some of the crude theories of political speculators. Thus, sample surveys established that people did, indeed, appear to vote their pocketbooks. Yet the demonstration created its embarrassments because it also established that exceptions to the rule were numerous. Not all factory workers, for example, voted alike. How was the behavior of the deviants from "group interest" to be explained? Refinement after refinement of theory and analysis added complexity to the original simple explanation. By introducing a bit of psychological theory it could be demonstrated that factory workers with optimistic expectations tended less to be governed by pocketbook considerations than did those whose outlook was gloomy. When a little social psychology was stirred into the analysis, it could be established that identifications formed early in life, such as attachments to political parties, also reinforced or resisted the pull of the interest of the moment. A sociologist, bringing to play the conceptual tools of his trade, then could show that those factory workers who associate intimately with like-minded persons on the average vote with greater solidarity than do social isolates. Inquiries conducted with great ingenuity along many such lines have enormously broadened our knowledge of the factors associated with the responses of people to the stimuli presented to them by political campaigns.[1]

Yet, by and large, the picture of the voter that emerges from a combination of the folklore of practical politics and the findings of the new electoral studies is not a pretty one. It is not a portrait of citizens moving to considered decision as they play their solemn role of making and unmaking governments. The older tradition from practical politics may regard the voter as an erratic and irrational fellow susceptible to manipulation by skilled humbugs. One need not live through many campaigns to observe

---

1. The principal books are: Paul F. Lazarsfeld, Bernard Berelson, and Hazel Gaudet, *The People's Choice* (New York: Duell, Sloan and Pearce, 1944); Angus Campbell, Gerald Gurin, and Warren E. Miller, *The Voter Decides* (Evanston, Ill.: Row, Peterson, 1954); Bernard R. Berelson, Paul F. Lazarsfeld, and William N. McPhee, *Voting* (Chicago: University of Chicago Press, 1954); Angus Campbell, Philip E. Converse, Warren E. Miller, and Donald E. Stokes, *The American Voter* (New York: Wiley, 1960). The periodical literature is almost limitless. The footnotes in Robert E. Lane's *Political Life* (Glencoe, Ill.: Free Press, 1959) constitute a handy guide to most of it.

politicians, even successful politicians, who act as though they regarded the people as manageable fools. Nor does a heroic conception of the voter emerge from the new analyses of electoral behavior. They can be added up to a conception of voting not as a civic decision but as an almost purely deterministic act. Given knowledge of certain characteristics of a voter—his occupation, his residence, his religion, his national origin, and perhaps certain of his attitudes—one can predict with a high probability the direction of his vote. The actions of persons are made to appear to be only predictable and automatic responses to campaign stimuli.

Most findings of the analysts of voting never travel beyond the circle of the technicians; the popularizers, though, give wide currency to the most bizarre—and most dubious—theories of electoral behavior. Public-relations experts share in the process of dissemination as they sell their services to politicians (and succeed in establishing that politicians are sometimes as gullible as businessmen). Reporters pick up the latest psychological secret from campaign managers and spread it through a larger public. Thus, at one time a goodly proportion of the literate population must have placed some store in the theory that the electorate was a pushover for a candidate who projected an appropriate "father image." At another stage, the "sincere" candidate supposedly had an overwhelming advantage. And even so kindly a gentleman as General Eisenhower was said to have an especial attractiveness to those of authoritarian personality within the electorate.

Conceptions and theories of the way voters behave do not raise solely arcane problems to be disputed among the democratic and antidemocratic theorists or questions to be settled by the elegant techniques of the analysts of electoral behavior. Rather, they touch upon profound issues at the heart of the problem of the nature and work-ability of systems of popular government. Obviously the perceptions of the behavior of the electorate held by political leaders, agitators, and activists condition, if they do not fix, the types of appeals politicians employ as they seek popular support. These perceptions—or theories—affect the nature of the input to the echo chamber, if we may revert to our earlier figure, and thereby control its output. They may govern, too, the kinds of actions that governments take as they look forward to the next election. If politicians perceive the electorate as responsive to father images, they will give it father images. If they see voters as most certainly responsive to nonsense, they will give them nonsense. If they see voters as susceptible to delusion, they will delude them. If they see an electorate receptive to the cold, hard realities, they will give it the cold, hard realities.

In short, theories of how voters behave acquire importance not because of their effects on voters, who may proceed blithely unaware of them. They gain significance because of their effects, both potentially and in reality, on candidates and other political leaders. If leaders believe the route to victory is by projection of images and cultivation of styles rather than by advocacy of policies to cope with the problems of the country, they will project images and cultivate styles to the neglect of the substance of politics. They will abdicate their prime function in a democratic system, which amounts, in essence, to the assumption of the risk of trying to persuade us to lift ourselves by our bootstraps.

Among the literary experts on politics there are those who contend that, because of the development of tricks for the manipulation of the masses, practices of political leadership in the management of voters have moved far toward the conversion of election campaigns into obscene parodies of the models set up by democratic idealists. They point to the good old days when politicians were deep thinkers, eloquent orators, and farsighted statesmen. Such estimates of the course of change in social institutions must be regarded with reserve. They may be only manifestations of the inverted optimism of aged and melancholy men who, estopped from hope for the future, see in the past a satisfaction of their yearning for greatness in our political life.

Whatever the trends may have been, the perceptions that leadership elements of democracies hold of the modes of response of the electorate must always be a matter of fundamental significance. Those perceptions determine the nature of the voice of the people, for they determine the character of the input into the echo chamber. While the output may be governed by the nature of the input, over the longer run the properties of the echo chamber may themselves be altered. Fed a steady diet of buncombe, the people may come to expect and to respond with highest predictability to buncombe. And those leaders most skilled in the propagation of buncombe may gain lasting advantage in the recurring struggles for popular favor.

The perverse and unorthodox argument of this little book is that voters are not fools. To be sure, many individual voters act in odd ways indeed; yet in the large the electorate behaves about as rationally and responsibly as we should expect, given the clarity of the alternatives presented to it and the character of the information available to it. In American presidential campaigns of recent decades the portrait of the American electorate that develops from the data is not one of an electorate straitjacketed by social determinants or moved by subconscious urges triggered by devilishly skillful propagandists. It is rather one of an electorate moved by concern about cen-

7

tral and relevant questions of public policy, of governmental performance, and of executive personality. Propositions so uncompromisingly stated inevitably represent overstatements. Yet to the extent that they can be shown to resemble the reality, they are propositions of basic importance for both the theory and the practice of democracy.

To check the validity of this broad interpretation of the behavior of voters, attention will center on the movements of voters across party lines as they reacted to the issues, events, and candidates of presidential campaigns between 1936 and 1960. Some Democratic voters of one election turned Republican at the next; others stood pat. Some Republicans of one presidential season voted Democratic four years later; others remained loyal Republicans. What motivated these shifts, sometimes large and sometimes small, in voter affection? How did the standpatters differ from the switchers? What led them to stand firmly by their party preference of four years earlier? Were these actions governed by images, moods, and other irrelevancies; or were they expressions of judgments about the sorts of questions that, hopefully, voters will weigh as they responsibly cast their ballots? On these matters evidence is available that is impressive in volume, if not always so complete or so precisely relevant as hindsight would wish. If one perseveres through the analysis of this extensive body of information, the proposition that the voter is not so irrational a fellow after all may become credible.[2]

2. The discussion in these chapters must be limited strictly to the data, which concern presidential voting only. The voter, as he chooses other candidates, acts on the basis of widely varying quantities of information; and campaign stimuli of widely differing clarity engage his attention in widely varying degree. The data for systematic study of voting for nonpresidential office, if they were available, would doubtless reveal the voter in roles both of bewilderment and of wisdom.

CHAPTER 2

STANDPATTERS,
SWITCHERS,
NEW VOTERS

The hullabaloo of a presidential campaign so commands our attention that we ascribe to campaigns great power to sway the multitude. Campaigning does change votes and it does bestir people to vote. Yet other influences doubtless outweigh the campaign in the determination of the vote. As voters mark their ballots they may have in their minds impressions of the last TV political spectacular of the campaign, but, more important, they have in their minds recollections of their experiences of the past four years. Those memories may be happy ones or they may be memories of dissatisfaction with what government has done or has left undone.

The impact of events from the inauguration of an Administration to the onset of the next presidential campaign may affect far more voters than the fireworks of the campaign itself. Governments must act or not act, and action or inaction may convert supporters into opponents or opponents into supporters. Events, over which government may, or more likely may not, have control, shape the attitudes of voters to the advantage or disadvantage of the party in power. By the time the presidential campaign rolls around the die may have been cast. The events between the 1936 election and the 1940 presidential conventions changed over twice as many votes as all the events of the 1940 campaign, Paul Lazarsfeld found in his noted study of Erie County, Ohio.[1] The Democrats had lost the election of 1952 by the time Eisenhower won the Republican nomination in July. That fate befell them in large measure through desertions by their 1948 supporters, according to persuasive evidence presented by Angus Campbell.[2]

Obviously, if we are to see whether the voter may after all try to form sensible judgments on those questions relevant to his supposed duties as a citizen, we need to analyze the movement of voters across party lines from presidential election to presidential election. Over a four-year period what kinds of people and how many desert their party to align themselves with the opposition and why? This shifting sector of the electorate must play a basic role in the workings of a democratic system, for the fear of loss of popular support powerfully disciplines the actions of governments.

The numbers of voters whose electoral affections remain the same from election to election measure the success of governments in retaining popular support—and of the outs in maintaining the solidarity of their ranks. These voters, too, make a decision—a decision to stand pat. They may behave quite as rationally as do voters with

1. Paul F. Lazarsfeld, Bernard Berelson, and Hazel Gaudet, *The People's Choice* (New York: Duell, Sloan and Pearce, 1944), p. 102.

2. Angus Campbell, Gerald Gurin, and Warren E. Miller, *The Voter Decides* (Evanston, Ill.: Row, Peterson, 1954), pp. 14-15.

transient party attachments, though popular political philosophy ascribes high virtue to the gyrations of the independent. On the other hand, the standpatter's perceptual filters may enable him to see in the stream of events only a reinforcement for a partisan attachment with roots that tie back to his childhood. It is quite as important to sense the motivation of the standpatter as it is to comprehend the drives that push the shifting voter from party to party.

Who switches from party to party? Who stands pat? Why? The information on which answers to these questions may be based is by no means easily obtained. Yet so essential is an understanding of the problem of getting the necessary facts that a few pages must be devoted to an indication of the nature and limits of the available data. These preliminary digressions will also afford opportunity to show the broad division of the electorate between standpatters and switchers and to indicate roughly the size of the group of new voters at each election.

Election statistics can tell us nothing about the movements of voters to and fro across party lines; they give only a net measure of changes in the party division from election to election. To trace changes or to identify continuities in voter sentiment over time one must employ some variant of the sample survey. By a panel study—a technique invented by Paul Lazarsfeld—one could interview the members of the same sample of voters at intervals over a period of time and follow changes or continuities in their individual voting preferences and other attitudes. The application of this technique to a national sample requires large resources and encounters the practical problem of attrition in the sample. If one begins with a sample of 2,000 persons and interviews them at intervals over a period of several years, the dropout, that is, persons who move and cannot be located plus mortality, mounts and creates problems in the interpretation of analyses of the surviving sample.[3]

Another way to follow changes in voter outlook is simply to ask the respondent in a pre-election interview how he voted four years earlier. The interview also yields an expression of current voting preference which, along with other information obtained in the interview, permits identification of the kinds of people shifting their voting preference and characteristics associated with these changes. This book rests largely on such recall data, which have their shortcomings, as will be shown, but they have the incontestable virtue of being available—and of being the only information covering so long a period of time.

Beginning in its 1940 election polls the American Institute of Public Opinion (AIPO)—Dr. George Gallup's organization—has asked its respondents for a recall of their vote of four years earlier. The wording of the question has differed somewhat from election to election. The form of the inquiry in 1960 was as follows: "In the election in November, 1956—when Eisenhower ran against Stevenson—did things come up which kept you from voting, or did you happen to vote? For whom?" In a 1944 survey the question put was: "Do you remember FOR CERTAIN whether or not you voted in the 1940 presidential election?" If the respondent had voted, he was asked: "Did you vote for Willkie, Roosevelt or Thomas?" Since Dr. Gallup has conducted several national surveys preceding each presidential election, the data on recall of past vote and on current voting intentions from 1940 through 1960 fill a massive collection of IBM cards. In

3. The Survey Research Center of the University of Michigan has in preparation a report of the findings of a panel study of a national sample extending over three presidential elections.

addition, the Roper poll, the National Opinion Research Center (NORC), and other survey organizations have occasionally collected similar data of which use will be made.

The skeptic may distrust a person's recall of his vote of four years ago. Commonly, even in surveys immediately after an election, a larger percentage claims to have voted for the winner than possibly could have, if the official election returns are assumed to be reasonably accurate measures of the vote.[4] Is not a greater overrecall of the vote for the winner to be expected after four years have elapsed? Or, if the winner turns out to be not so popular, should we expect error on the low side? Or do we have a source of error in the tendency of some people to say that they have voted when they actually did not inconvenience themselves by the performance of that civic duty?

If the division of the remembered vote approximates the actual division of the vote four years earlier, some faith can be placed in the recall data. Table 2.1 compares the two sets of figures for the elections from 1936 through 1960. As they reported their earlier votes, the respondents to poll questions recorded a preference for the winner from 2.5 to 9.2 percentage points higher than his actual vote. The 1948 recall of the 1944 Roosevelt vote exceeded by 9.2 points the actual vote; in 1956 the overrecall of the 1952 vote for Eisenhower was 8.6 points. These were the widest overstatements of the earlier actual vote in the series. Yet among those with a presidential preference at the times of these two surveys—and these are the cases that must be used in our analyses—the overrecall was

4. The error in recall immediately after the election is not always embarrassingly wide. Thus, in mid-November, 1960, the AIPO sample reported a vote of 50.4 per cent for Kennedy.

smaller, 4.2 and 5.2 points respectively. Perhaps those undecided at the time of the surveys in 1948 and 1952 included a disproportionate number of persons who erroneously represented themselves as having voted for

TABLE 2.1. Recall of presidential vote of four years earlier by respondents in national sample, compared with actual vote, 1936–1960

Year of survey	Recall of vote in:	Per cent of 2-party vote to winning presidential candidate			Overrecall (percentage point difference)
		Recall in AIPO survey	N^a	Actual vote	
1940	1936	65[b]	(2,524)	62.5	2.5
1944	1940	58[c]	(2,480)	55.0	3.0
1948	1944	63[d]	(2,219)	53.8	9.2
1952	1948	60[e]	(2,062)	52.3	7.7
1956	1952	64[f]	(1,521)	55.4	8.6
1960	1956	62[g]	(2,018)	57.8	4.2

[a] N is the number of poll respondents on which the preceding percentage is based. Thus, in this table, each figure in parentheses is the number of respondents who reported a recall of a vote for a major-party candidate at the presidential election of four years earlier. For example, in 1940, of those persons interviewed, 2,524 recalled how they voted in 1936; and 65 per cent of those 2,524 persons recalled that they had voted for the winning candidate.

[b] AIPO 221, 10-23-40. Roper 22, October 1940, also gave a 65 per cent Democratic recall of 1936.

[c] AIPO 334, 10-26-44. NORC 30/229 gave a Democratic percentage of 57 in the recall of 1940.

[d] AIPO 431, 10-14-48.

[e] AIPO 507-K, 10-15-52. AIPO 508-K, 11-12-52, produced a recall of 56 per cent Democratic in 1948. The 1952 Survey Research Center sample had a 58 per cent Democratic recall for 1948. See Angus Campbell, Gerald Gurin, and Warren E. Miller, *The Voter Decides* (Evanston, Ill.: Row, Peterson, 1954), p. 16.

[f] AIPO 573-K, 10-16-56. Roper 65, October 1956, showed a 64 per cent Republican recall for 1952.

[g] AIPO 637-K, 10-18-60.

the winner four years earlier. The error, too, may not be as wide as our figures suggest. The recall is by that portion of the electorate of four years earlier who were still living and able to be interviewed; the voting behavior of these survivors may have diverged from that of the entire electorate. Thus, the Survey Research Center's panel data show a 1956 Eisenhower percentage of 61 among survivors who voted in 1960, a figure not unlike the 62 per cent recall by these persons in the Gallup data.[5] Whatever the explanation for overrecall—and it probably differs from election to election—the recall of the vote is near enough to the reality to give us some confidence in the contrasts between groups of voters made in later chapters.[6]

As a framework for our subsequent detailed inquiries— and as an analysis of interest in its own right—we may at this point build from the data estimates of the gross features of the electorate as a whole as it shifts or maintains its position from election to election. From the simple figures of election results the impression develops that the electorate remains fairly static from election to election. Seemingly only a few voters shift one way or another to alter the partisan divisions slightly. Instead a vast and intricate churning about occurs as millions of voters switch party preferences. Millions more enter the active electorate; they have become of age or have de-

5. P. E. Converse, A. Campbell, W. E. Miller, and D. E. Stokes, "Stability and Change in 1960: A Reinstating Election," *American Political Science Review*, 55 (1961), 272.
6. Table 2.1 also shows a high overrecall in 1952 of the 1948 vote for President Harry Truman. A similar discrepancy occurred in the Survey Research Center's 1952 national sample. The overstatement in its sample was especially high among Southern voters, a phenomenon said to be probably attributable to an understandable reticence among Southerners about confessing to having voted for Dewey in 1948. See Angus Campbell *et al.*, *The Voter Decides*, pp. 6-7.

cided to vote this time after not having voted for one reason or another at the previous election.

The body of voters at any single election consists principally of three major components. Standpatters make up the largest single component; they are those voters who cast their ballots for candidates of the same political party at two successive elections. The switchers are another group, considerably smaller than the standpatters, but still they number in the millions. This category, of course, consists of two kinds of voters, one moving across party lines in one direction and the other shifting in the opposite direction. New voters make up a third component, which consists of those who were too young to vote at the preceding election or who did not happen to vote then. Throughout the discussion attention will be focused on the characteristics and behaviors of these three major types of voters. At the moment the purpose is simply to present estimates of the size of these elements of the electorate.[7]

Shifting voters are more numerous than is commonly supposed. Election returns subtly but erroneously suggest that they are few in number. One may note that Eisenhower polled 55.4 per cent of the major-party vote in 1952 and 57.8 per cent in 1956. Then one may slip easily into the belief that from 1952 to 1956 only 2.4 per cent of the 1952 voters changed their allegiance; in fact, five or six times as large a proportion switched their preference. The figure of 2.4 is a measure of net change resulting from shifts from Democratic to Republican and from Republican to Democratic

7. The meticulous student may be unhappy because the analysis ignores other categories of voters. Thus, no heed is paid to voters who shift from a major party to a minor party or vice versa. The inclusion of these and other such categories would complicate the analysis without materially affecting the findings.

and the addition of new voters to each side (as well as the subtraction of former voters from each side); it is a figure that conceals more than it reveals.

The switchers at individual elections over the period 1940–1960 probably ranged in number from about one eighth to about one fifth, or slightly more, of the survivors from those who had voted at the preceding election. The dimensions of the gross shift from party to party from election to election over that period are shown by Table 2.2. The data of the table also suggest some of the difficulties of measuring shift and some of the limitations of our data. The shift in preference, as estimated from pre-election polls, usually differs from the shift in vote, as reported in polls taken immediately following the election. The widest of these differences turns up in the 1948 pre-election and post-election surveys, the year of the great unhappiness of the pollsters. These discrepancies reflect voting shifts in the last days of the campaign not caught by the pre-election polls as well as nonvoting by some of those who had expressed a preference in pre-election polls.[8] The variations in size of the shifting bloc of voters from election to election are doubtless produced to some degree by changes in data-collection practices. Nevertheless, the peaks in size of this group, about one fifth in 1952 and in 1960, lend plausibility to the broad contours of the data;

8. Several inquiries suggest that an effect of the campaigns of 1940, 1944, and 1948 was to arouse, to mobilize, and to crystallize the intentions of Democratic voters. Hence, pre-election surveys for these elections probably overstate the rate of switching from Democratic to Republican that actually occurred in the voting. Apparently by the time of the polling some of the Democrats who had considered switching had been brought into line with the party. The 1956 pre-election data suggest that pre-election intentions to switch may tend to exceed the actual defection rates for an incumbent party that wins re-election, be it Democratic or Republican.

high proportions of shifters would be expected in these elections of party turnover.[9]

If from one eighth to one fifth of the voters shift in their party preferences, the reciprocals of these fractions estimate the proportions of standpatters within the electorate. Of those voters at one election who survive until the next and vote, from four fifths to seven eighths are standpatters, that is, they vote for the candidate of the party they supported at the preceding election. For these individuals, editorial writers and other journeyman political philosophers reserve their most severe scorn. It may be quite as sensible, though, to remain steadfast in one's party loyalty as to move across party lines. In any event a certain caution is prudent if one is tempted to look with scorn on so many people. Probably more than 45 million of the 68 million or so persons who voted in 1960 cast their ballot for the presidential candidate of the same party they had supported in 1956. Nor do our data enable us to say that persons remain standpatters for more than two successive elections. Standpatters at one election may be shifters in the next. It would be an error to suppose that switchers are eternally volatile and the standpatters forever stable.

An unfortunately named category, "new voters," makes up another component of the electorate. It consists of those who were too young to vote at the preceding election and those who admitted that they had not managed to vote. These persons made up roughly 15 to 20 per cent

9. S. J. Eldersveld long ago called attention to the size and significance of the bloc of shifting voters. See his "The Independent Vote: Measurement, Characteristics, and Implications for Party Strategy," *American Political Science Review*, 46 (1952), 732-753. In a more recent study H. Daudt takes the students of electoral behavior to task because of their neglect of the floating voter. See *Floating Voters and the Floating Vote* (Leiden: Stenfert Kroese, 1961).

TABLE 2.2. Percentages of those who voted in preceding presidential election shifting in preference and in reported vote from one major party to the other

Period of shift	In pre-election preference	N[a]	In post-election report of vote	N[a]
1936–40	17[b]	(12,031)	16[c]	(4,319)
1940–44	14[d]	(12,086)	11[e]	(1,673)
1944–48	18[f]	(5,223)	13[g]	(1,795)
1948–52	17[h]	(6,120)	20[i]	(1,795)
1952–56	13[j]	(2,789)	[k]	[k]
1956–60	21[l]	(4,295)	22[m]	(1,857)

[a] As in other tables, the numbers in parentheses are the numbers of poll respondents on which the percentages are based. To illustrate: before the 1940 election 12,031 respondents expressed a preference for one of the major-party candidates and recalled how they had voted in 1936, and 17 per cent of these 12,031 persons had switched their party preference. Similarly, 4,319 poll respondents interviewed *after* the 1940 election recalled how they voted in both elections, and 16 per cent of them indicated they had switched.

[b] A consolidation of AIPO 217, 10-22-40; 220, 10-22-40; 221, 10-23-40; 218-K, 10-24-40; 219-K, 10-24-40. Roper 22, October 1940, produced a gross shift in preference of 14 per cent.

[c] A consolidation of AIPO 224-K, 11-19-40, and 225-K, 11-19-40.

[d] A consolidation of AIPO 330, 10-3-44; 331, 10-6-44; 332, 10-12-44; 333, 10-17-44; and 334, 10-26-44. NORC 30/229, October 1944, showed a gross shift in preference of 10 per cent.

[e] AIPO 335, 11-15-44.

[f] A consolidation of AIPO 429, 9-28-48; 430, 10-5-48; 431, 10-14-48.

[g] AIPO 432, 11-1-48.

[h] A consolidation of AIPO 504-K, 10-1-52; 505-TPS, 10-3-52; 506-K, 10-7-52; 507-K, 10-15-52.

[i] AIPO 508-K, 11-12-52. Survey Research Center data also yielded a recalled turnover rate of 20 per cent. Computed from data presented by Angus Campbell, "Surge and Decline: A Study of Electoral Change," *Public Opinion Quarterly*, 24 (1960), 407.

[j] A consolidation of AIPO 572-K, 10-5-56, and AIPO 573-K, 10-16-56. Roper 65, October 1956, turned up a gross shift in preference of 12 per cent.

[k] The 1956 AIPO post-election schedule did not include a question on the 1952 vote.

[l] A consolidation of AIPO 636-K, 9-26-60, and 637-K, 10-18-60.

[m] AIPO 638-K, 11-15-60. The Survey Research Center's panel showed a gross shift of 23 per cent. See P. E. Converse, A. Campbell, W. E. Miller, and D. E. Stokes, "Stability and Change in 1960: A Reinstating Election," *American Political Science Review*, 55 (1961), 272.

TABLE 2.3. Contribution of new voters, shifters, and stand-patters to pre-election major-party presidential preference and to post-election report of vote[a]

Election	New voters[b]	Shifters[c]	Stand-patters[d]	Total
1940				
Pre-election preference[e]	16%	14%	70%	100%
Post-election report	16	13	71	100
1944				
Pre-election preference[f]	15	13	72	100
Post-election report	13	10	77	100
1948				
Pre-election preference	23	14	63	100
Post-election report	16	11	73	100
1952				
Pre-election preference	30	12	58	100
Post-election report[g]	20	16	64	100
1956				
Pre-election preference[h]	27	10	63	100
Post-election report[i]	—	—	—	—
1960				
Pre-election preference	27	15	58	100
Post-election report	14	19	67	100

[a] Based on same surveys as comparable items of Table 2.2.

[b] Those with a preference or a vote for a major-party candidate who had been either too young to vote in the preceding election or had not happened to vote then.

[c] Those reporting a vote for a major-party candidate four years earlier and with a preference or a vote for the other major party in the current election.

[d] Those reporting a vote for a major-party candidate four years earlier and expressing a preference or reporting a vote for the candidate of the same party.

[e] Roper 22, October 1940, yielded the following percentages: new voters, 16; shifters, 12; standpatters, 72. The AIPO sample for 1940 differed slightly from the sample of later years. In that year the first question of the schedule asked whether the respondent was registered or planned to register. If registration was not required, the respondent was asked if he would be "eligible (able) to vote in (name of county or town) in the Presidential election this year?" The interviewer was instructed to discontinue the interview if the respondent would not be "able to vote." (*Table continued at top of next page*)

STANDPATTERS, SWITCHERS, NEW VOTERS

ᶠ NORC 30/229, October 1944, produced the following percentages: new voters, 12; shifters, 9; standpatters, 79. Interviews were conducted during the last four days of October.

ᵍ The Survey Research Center's sample produced the following percentages: new voters, 20; switchers, 16; standpatters, 64. Computed from data presented by Angus Campbell, "Surge and Decline: A Study of Electoral Change," *Public Opinion Quarterly*, 24 (1960), 407.

ʰ Roper 65, October 1956, showed the following percentages: new voters, 25; shifters, 9; standpatters, 66.

ⁱ Not available.

of the sample at each election from 1940 to 1960, as may be seen from Table 2.3. Ordinarily the proportions of new voters are higher among those expressing a preference in the pre-election surveys than among those reporting after the election that they had voted.[10] The high proportions of nonvoters among the "new voters" points to characteristics of this heterogeneous group that need to be kept clearly in mind as the analysis proceeds.

Among the "new voters" are those who have turned 21 and become eligible to vote since the preceding presidential election. In most of our pre-election samples, of those "new voters" with a presidential preference around 40 per cent are under 30 years of age. Nonvoting tends to be high in this age bracket; yet obviously the long-run fortunes of the parties depend mightily on their capacity to recruit new followers from among those entering the active electorate. The formation of party loyalties begins, of course, long before age 21. Many of those moving into the electorate come equipped with a sense of party identification; others remain to be recruited.

10. No attempt has been made to screen from the pre-election sample those persons with no intention of voting or those unlikely to vote. Hence, these tabulations are not precisely comparable with Gallup's published pre-election estimates. For the Gallup practice on this point, see Paul Perry, "Election Survey Procedures of the Gallup Poll," *Public Opinion Quarterly*, 24 (1960), 531-542, and "Gallup Poll Survey Experience, 1950 to 1960," *Public Opinion Quarterly*, 26 (1962), 272-279.

The "new voters" also include at all age levels many "in-and-out" voters, whose psychological characteristics may make them of special interest, if not invariably of special importance, in the behavior of the electorate. Some of the "in-and-out" voters were prevented from voting four years earlier by causes beyond their control. They had no legal residence; they were out of the country; they were ill; or for some other reason they could not make their way to the polls. Others, doubtless far more numerous, are persons with a low interest in politics, the apolitical, the apathetic, the indifferent, and those who vote only under the pressure of powerful stimuli or the exceptionally persuasive nudging of party workers. They are persons marginal to the political system who may be pulled into the election on the side of the party able under the circumstances of the moment to attract their attention or rouse their interest.

Though we commonly ascribe great significance to the switchers, they are in many elections outnumbered by the "new voters." In some elections, indeed, the "new voters" contribute significantly to the outcome, if they do not determine it. Hence, this group presents a continuing challenge to the contending parties, which must seek to recruit young voters and to arouse and attract support from among the "in-and-out" sector of the electorate to maintain their position. The significance of the group is suggested by the fact that in 1960 on the order of eight or nine million persons voted who had not voted in 1956.

Estimation of the magnitude of opposing movements of voters highlights another aspect of the gross behavior of the electorate. At the elections of 1940, 1944, and 1948 the Democratic defection rate was far more marked than the Republican rate, as Table 2.4 indicates. Over the presidential terms preceding these elections, the impact of Democratic policies, the hostile flow of communications, and other factors drove relatively large numbers of voters from the Democratic ranks to the support of the Republican candidate. On the other hand, the Republicans, whose support had shrunk to a hard core of dedicated partisans, lost comparatively few voters to the Democrats. The pre-election surveys, it will be noted, showed for these elections a higher rate of Democratic loss than did the post-election polls. Probably the best guess is that for these elections the actual proportions of shifters fell somewhere between the pre-election and post-election estimates shown in Table 2.4. In any case, the Democratic party over these years had to struggle to offset the loss of millions of supporters by attracting erstwhile Republican voters, by recruiting young voters, and by getting out to the polls older Democrats with irregular voting habits. On the other hand, by 1956 the pattern took a reverse form as the Republican party came to suffer defections at a higher rate than the Democratic party and sought to maintain its waning ranks by the recruitment of 1952 Democrats and new voters.

Our broad electoral components appear in another light when we examine the contribution of each type of voter to the total vote for each presidential candidate. The proportions of the vote for each candidate coming from standpatters, switchers, and new voters are shown in Table 2.5. Though the data generate the suspicion that the interview response probably results in an overstatement of the proportion of shifters, the patterns of composition of candidate support, when arrayed against the known characteristics of the elections covered, give us some confidence in the gross differences revealed by the data. Presentation

TABLE 2.4. Direction of movement of party shifters from one presidential election to the next, and divisions among new and old voters[a]

Period of shift	Per cent shifting		Per cent to winner	
	% of D's, D-R	% of R's, R-D	% of new voters[b]	% of those voting at preceding election
1936–40				
Pre-election preference	24 (7,871)	4 (4,160)	59 (2,231)	51
Post-election report[c]	23 (2,750)	5 (1,569)	56 (798)	51
1940–44				
Pre-election preference	18 (7,645)	7 (4,441)	55 (1,984)	50
Post-election report	14 (923)	8 (750)	57 (263)	51
1944–48				
Pre-election preference	28 (3,048)	3 (2,175)	52 (1,523)	43
Post-election report	15 (1,085)	9 (710)	64 (343)	55
1948–52				
Pre-election preference	26 (3,547)	6 (2,573)	51 (2,617)	55
Post-election report[d]	32 (985)	6 (810)	58 (446)	60
1952–56				
Pre-election preference	8 (1,898)	16 (3,551)	50 (1,042)	58
Post-election report[e]	—	—	—	—
1956–60				
Pre-election preference	9 (1,591)	28 (2,704)	54 (1,400)	51
Post-election report[f]	12 (696)	28 (1,161)	51 (301)	50

[a] Based on same surveys as Table 2.2. As in that table, the figures in parentheses are the numbers of poll respondents on which the percentages are based. For example, 7,871 respondents, when interviewed prior to the 1940 election, recalled voting Democratic in the 1936 election and expressed a preference for one of the major-party candidates in

1940. Of these respondents, 24 per cent had switched their preference to Republican.

ᵇ New voters include both those too young to vote at the preceding election and those who did not happen to vote.

ᶜ The post-election survey asked, in 1940 for example, both the 1940 and the 1936 vote. The post-election recall of the vote four years before did not usually differ substantially from the pre-election recall.

ᵈ The comparable percentages from data of the Survey Research Center were: D's, D-R, 32; R's, R-D, 4; new voters R, 55; those voting at preceding election R, 59. Computed from data presented by Angus Campbell, "Surge and Decline: A Study of Electoral Change," *Public Opinion Quarterly*, 24 (1960), 407.

ᵉ Not available. The 1956 pre-election survey shows, as it should, a heavier Eisenhower preference than the 1952 pre-election survey. Compared with the 1952 post-election survey, though, it shows a decline. A 1956 post-election survey probably would have shown a higher Eisenhower percentage than did the pre-election poll. That contrast prevailed in 1952.

ᶠ Roughly comparable figures from the Survey Research Center's data show 15 per cent of D's, D-R, and 28 per cent of R's, R-D. Derived from P. E. Converse, A. Campbell, W. E. Miller, and D. E. Stokes, "Stability and Change in 1960: A Reinstating Election," *American Political Science Review*, 55 (1961), 272, Table I.

of the data in percentages, though, may make us oblivious to the large absolute numbers involved. If we trust the percentages of the 1960 post-election poll, the distribution of the Kennedy vote among our three types of voters was approximately as follows:

Standpatters	19.1 million
Switchers	10.3 million
New voters	4.8 million

And the contributions of the three types of voters to the Nixon total were approximately as follows:

Standpatters	26.6 million
Switchers	2.7 million
New voters	4.8 million

One need not delude himself into the belief that these estimates are precise to regard them as within shouting distance of the realities. The outcome of the 1960 election makes it reasonable to suppose that the Eisenhower voters of 1956 who shifted to Kennedy outnumbered by far the Stevenson voters who moved over to Nixon, though the absolute numbers of switchers may have been fewer in number than the indicated total of 13 million.[11]

All these tabulations, roughly indicative of the proportions of the electorate falling into our three broad categories of voters, map the gross topography of the data which will be analyzed in more detail in succeeding chapters. The central concern will be with the behavior of those voters who move to and fro across party lines; yet their characteristics assume importance only by contrast with the standpatters and, to a lesser extent, the new voters. Hence almost equal attention must be given to the three types of voters. In this introductory reconnaissance both pre-election and post-election surveys have been used. Most of the subsequent analyses will depend on pre-election polls alone and, therefore, will reflect voting intentions rather than the vote as reported after the fact. In some of the analyses, too, the differences between contrasting groups of voters may be muted by the combination of several pre-election polls. If the extent of polarization between two groups increases during the

11. To match the figures in the text the disappearance of 1956 voters by 1960 would have to amount to about 3.3 million or 5.3 per cent of the 1956 voters. The dropout would consist principally of 1956 voters who became 1960 nonvoters and of loss by death. Mortality alone over the four-year period would account for considerably more than 5.3 per cent of those 55 and over in 1956. P. E. Converse, on the basis of the Survey Research Center's panel sample, reports that "somewhat less than 10 per cent of the eligible 1956 electorate had become effectively ineligible by 1960, with death as the principal cause." He defines "eligible electorate" as those noninstitutionalized citizens over 21. P. E. Converse, A. Campbell, W. E. Miller, and D. E. Stokes, "Stability and Change in 1960: A Reinstating Election," *American Political Science Review*, 55 (1961), 271.

campaign, the consolidation of several samples will reduce the apparent polarization. The reason for consolidation, though, is that it enables one to build up the cells of the sample to a sufficient size to permit estimates of the behavior of small groups within the electorate. If five of fifteen 1956 Negro Republican voters turning up in a single sample were Democratic in 1960, not a great deal

TABLE 2.5. Composition of vote for major-party presidential candidates, according to voting record at preceding election[a]

	Democratic			Republican		
Year	Stand-patters	Shifters	New voters	Stand-patters	Shifters	New voters
1940						
Pre-election	80%	2%	18%	58%	28%	14%
Post-election	80	3	17	61	25	14
1944						
Pre-election	80	4	16	64	22	14
Post-election	79	6	15	74	14	12
1948						
Pre-election	73	3	24	58	23	19
Post-election	77	5	18	69	18	13
1952						
Pre-election	65	4	31	52	19	29
Post-election[b]	74	5	21	57	23	20
1956						
Pre-election	52	17	31	72	4	24
Post-election[c]	—	—	—	—	—	—
1960						
Pre-election	46	24	30	71	6	23
Post-election	56	30	14	78	8	14

[a] This table is based on the same surveys as Table 2.2, and the categories of voters are defined as in Table 2.3.

[b] The Survey Research Center's sample yielded for the Democratic vote the following proportions: 75, 4, 21; for the Republican, 56, 25, 19. Computed from data presented by Angus Campbell, "Surge and Decline: A Study of Electoral Change," *Public Opinion Quarterly*, 24 (1960), 407.

[c] Not available.

of faith can be placed in a statement that 33 per cent switched. If, however, by the addition of several surveys a larger sample of 1956 Negro Republicans can be obtained, we may have more confidence that the differences between their behavior and that of other groups of 1956 voters actually existed in the entire electorate, even though the measures of these differences may be inexact.

MAINTAINING THE NEW DEAL COALITION

The apparent stability of the popular support of the political party dominant at the moment excites the curiosity of students of American politics. For relatively long periods one party or the other commands so consistently the votes of a majority that the country is said to be either normally Republican or normally Democratic. From 1932 to 1952 elections appeared to be only reassertions by the standing majority of its continued faith in Democratic leadership. In 1932 Franklin D. Roosevelt drew 59.1 per cent of the two-party vote and in 1936, in an extraordinary expression of popular confidence, 62.5 per cent. The Democratic proportion of the vote declined in succeeding elections bit by bit: 55.0 per cent in 1940; 53.8 per cent in 1944; and 52.3 per cent in 1948. Yet it seemed as if each election was but an occasion for the New Deal to muster again its phalanxes only in slightly diminished strength, march them to the polls, and thereby record its claim to power for another four years.

Elections such as these, in which the party pattern of the preceding election prevails, Angus Campbell calls "maintaining" elections.[1] While this characterization serves happily in a conceptual system for the differentiation of broad types of elections, it tells us nothing about the processes by which a majority party maintains—or does not maintain—its dominance. A satisfactory explanation of those processes would move us toward a better understanding of popular government. Such evidence as can be mustered suggests that the popular majority does not hold together like a ball of sticky popcorn. Rather, no sooner has a popular majority been constructed than it begins to crumble. The maintenance of a supportive majority requires governmental actions, policies, and gestures that reinforce the confidence of those who have placed their faith in the Administration. Yet to govern is to antagonize not only opponents but also at least some supporters; as the loyalty of one group is nourished, another group may be repelled. A series of maintaining elections occurs only in consequence of a complex process of interaction between government and populace in which old friends are sustained, old enemies are converted into new friends, old friends become even bitter opponents, and new voters are attracted to the cause—all in proper proportions to produce repeatedly for the dominant party its apparently stable and continuing majority.

The unbroken series of Democratic victories in the 1930's and 1940's occurred against a background of marked and abrupt innovations in governmental policy. To the extent that interactions between governmental action and public attitudes can be traced, this epoch should be instructive about the processes involved in the maintenance and renewal of a dominant popular coalition. And,

1. Angus Campbell, P. E. Converse, W. E. Miller, and D. E. Stokes, *The American Voter* (New York: Wiley, 1960), ch. 19.

thereby, we may also enlarge our information on the behavior of the supposedly errant voter. To speak of these interactions, though, we must recall some of the principal governmental actions of the 1930's. For a substantial part of the population they are by now only vague episodes in a dim and distant history.

The federal government underwent a radical transformation after the Democratic victory of 1932. It had been a remote authority with a limited range of activity. It operated the postal system, improved rivers and harbors, maintained armed forces on a scale fearsome only to banana republics, and performed other functions of which the average citizen was hardly aware. Within a brief time it became an institution that affected intimately the lives and fortunes of most, if not all, citizens. Measures of recovery and of reform—as the categorization of the time went—contributed to this fundamental alteration of federal activities. Legislative endeavors to achieve economic recovery from the Great Depression shaded over into steps toward basic reform; both types of policy touched the interests and hopes of great numbers of people and ignited the fiercest political controversy.

Large-scale measures for the relief of the unemployed made federal policy highly perceptible to millions of destitute persons. Administered at first as direct relief—a dole —by state relief administrations, the program soon came to be conducted by the Works Progress Administration, a federal agency which employed people on projects as diverse as theatricals, road construction, and leaf raking to the accompaniment of a spirited criticism not noticeably shared by those who relied on the WPA for sustenance. Another numerous class of persons received federal assistance through the Home Owners' Loan Corporation, an agency which had $3,000,000,000 to refinance home

31

mortgages to tide necessitous debtors over until a better day. Hard-pressed banks and other business enterprises received infusions of government capital often in the form of loans. Expenditures on a new scale for public works pumped money into the economy. By the Agricultural Adjustment Act, Congress attempted to alleviate the lot of the farmer who had been especially hard hit by the depression. The National Recovery Administration sought, oddly enough, to activate industry by something of a system of legalized cartels, with the inclusion in the cartel agreements (or industry codes) of standards with respect to minimum wages, maximum hours, collective bargaining, and other aspects of the employer-employee relationship.

Only a hazy line divided measures of recovery from those of reform; yet some actions clearly contemplated permanent and often drastic changes in public policy. Some of these new policies had effects of marked visibility. The Social Security Act of 1935 established a system of federal grants to states for programs of assistance to the aged, to the blind, and to dependent children, but it also instituted a system of contributory old-age annuities and a scheme of unemployment compensation, the first national steps into the field of social insurance. The Wagner Labor Relations Act assured to labor the right to organize and imposed on employers an obligation to bargain with employees collectively, an act of fundamental significance in the definition of the structure of the industrial order. In another area the government hoped by the Public Utility Holding Company Act to prevent a recurrence of financial abuses that had been notable, and the Tennessee Valley Authority and various power projects were regarded by the electrical utilities as an entering wedge for a socialism that would ultimately destroy them. Other legislation restrained sharp operators in the securities business who had bilked a goodly number of their fellow men in the halcyon days of the new era of the 1920's.

The merits or demerits of all these actions—and many others—are not our concern. The relevance of their mention is to suggest the considerable range of novel governmental actions with a widespread impact upon the fortunes and aspirations of voters. What kinds of interactions between government and electorate occurred in consequence of this revolution—as American revolutions go—in public policy? The broad effect was, of course, obvious. By 1936 the innovative period of the New Deal had pretty well run its course, and in that year the voters responded with a resounding ratification of the new thrust of governmental policy. Or, if one wishes to be cautious, the electorate resoundingly rejected the Republican alternative, which, as the campaign of 1936 developed, appeared to be a hysterical plea to return to the pre-1932 status quo lest the American system become a dictatorship.[2]

To portray the processes of the maintenance of the New Deal coalition, though, one must go beyond the broad electoral verdict and examine the detailed movements in voter sentiment underlying the grand totals. The maintenance and switching of party positions reflected in part responses to specific and concrete actions of government; they also reflected the responses of voters to the political oratory of the time. As campaigns developed, the commotion over individual policies seemed to be transmuted into the grand abstractions of political debate. The political discussion of the 1930's was heavily tinged with the rhetoric of the conflict of class and interest, and the

2. For the tenor of the politics of the time, see A. M. Schlesinger, Jr., *The Politics of Upheaval* (Boston: Houghton Mifflin, 1960).

battle seemed to take the shape of a competition between rich and poor, or between the American constitutional system and some alien alternative. On the left, evangels, such as Huey Long, preached a doctrine of "share the wealth," while those who had somewhat more than a modicum of wealth organized the Liberty League and other such societies to defend the American system. In 1936 the Republican national committee gloomily forecast that the "American plan of government might be lost forever," if Roosevelt were kept in office.

How might voters be expected to respond to the actions of government and to the campaign oratory of this era? American parties have had historically a multiclass following. Doubtless in 1932, though the data are not available, persons of all classes deserted the Republicans to vote for Franklin D. Roosevelt and a change. The result was that the 1932 Democratic vote probably included large numbers of persons who would not be regarded as "Democratic" in disposition. At any rate, it would be plausible to expect that as the New Deal unfolded, persons of upper-class status and of conservative disposition would be drawn from their Democratic posture to the Republican ranks. Moreover, it might be supposed that a counter-tendency would also operate as 1932 Republican voters in the lesser economic categories moved over to the Democratic side of the fence. In short, the impact of governmental actions and political rhetoric would be expected to heighten polarization along class and occupational lines.

Some such movement of voters occurred, evidently on a fairly large scale. Many upper-class Democratic voters defected, while relatively fewer working-class Democrats left the ranks. Scarcely any information is available for the election of 1936, but in the elections of 1940, 1944, and

1948 these differentials in party switching existed. Persons at all economic levels at each election moved away from the Democratic party but at rates varying with level of economic status. The differentials in party defection among economic levels, as estimated from Gallup polls of presidential preference, appear in Table 3.1. The rankings from "wealthy" to "poor" assigned by the interviewers are doubtless not measures of precision; nevertheless, of the "wealthy" 1936 Democratic voters, in the neighborhood

TABLE 3.1. Patterns of vote switching in presidential elections, 1936–1948, in relation to economic status[a]

	1936–40[b]		1940–44[c]		1944–48[d]	
Status	% of 1936 D's, D-R	% of 1936 R's, R-D	% of 1940 D's, D-R	% of 1940 R's, R-D	% of 1944 D's, D-R	% of 1944 R's, R-D
Wealthy	46	2	35	4	e	0
Average +	30	1	27	5	47	1
Average	28	4	24	7	32	3
Poor +	20	5	f	f	f	f
Poor	18	7	19	8	22	6
Old-age assistance	19	4	13	5	18	e
On relief	14	7	11	e	e	e

a The table entries are the percentages of those with a recall of a vote for a major-party candidate at the first election of the pair of years who expressed a preference for a major-party candidate in surveys in October just prior to the election of the second year of each pair. In each instance several surveys are combined to obtain larger samples in the individual cells. Economic status was that assigned to the respondent by the AIPO interviewer.

b A consolidation of the following AIPO surveys: 215K, 216T, 217, 218K. Roper 22, October 1940, yielded the following percentages of switchers, D-R, in the indicated economic levels: A, 25; B, 24; C, 20; D, 12. The corresponding R-D switches were: 2, 3, 5, 9.

c A consolidation of AIPO 330, 331, 332, 333, 334.

d A consolidation of AIPO 430 and 431.

e Less than 50 cases.

f Data obtained from low-income respondents in 1944 and 1948 were coded only in terms of a "poor" category. There was no "poor +" category.

of four out of ten deserted to the Republicans in 1940. At the other extreme, less than one in seven persons on relief took that step.

The countermovement, from Republican in 1936 to Democratic in 1940, was relatively small, yet it had a class bias in that relatively more of the poor than of the better-off 1936 Republicans switched to Democratic in 1940. In 1944 involvement in World War II gave the stimuli of the campaign a less class-oriented tone; yet in lesser degree than in 1940 the same class-tinged pattern of party switching prevailed. In 1948, with the war out of the way, the political battle assumed its older form with a more marked difference in switching among economic levels. Though the rates of switching in party preference shown by the pre-election polls analyzed in Table 3.1 may exceed the switch in the actual vote, they suggest the existence of quite large movements across party lines in these elections which brought voting alignments toward a closer congruity with income classes.[3]

Another test of our expectations about how voters might have responded to the impact of the New Deal appears in Table 3.2, which shows the switches from Democratic to Republican within broad occupational groups at the same series of elections. Business and professional Democratic

3. For the technician it should be noted that the differences in switching rates that appear, for example, in the first column of Table 3.1 could be attributable in part to a variant of the Maccobyean effect, so called for its identification by Eleanor Maccoby, "Pitfalls in the Analysis of Panel Data: A Research Note on Some Technical Aspects of Voting," *American Journal of Sociology*, 61 (1956), 359-362. The effect may result in an overstatement of differences in rates of change between large and small samples. Random errors in recording responses and in punching data into cards may inflate the rates of change for small N's more than for large N's. The odds are that the potential of the effect is negligible for most of our tables, but comparisons between cells with large and with extremely small N's should be regarded with some wariness.

voters at one election were far more likely to defect to the Republican candidate at the next election than were unskilled workers. Nevertheless, defections occurred at all occupational levels, a matter not easily explained if one attributes voting behavior largely to the effect of objective economic interest. If one's concern as an unskilled worker governs his voting, by what conceivable reason should an unskilled Democrat of 1936 have become a Republican voter in 1940? The explanation, which will occupy us later, is not immediately apparent; nevertheless, about one in seven of the group in question made that switch. Table 3.2 incidentally illustrates some of the char-

TABLE 3.2. Percentages within occupational categories switching from Democratic to Republican presidential preference from election to election, 1936–1948, as measured by pre-election and post-election polls[a]

Group	1936–40[b] Pre	1936–40[b] Post	1940–44[c] Pre	1940–44[c] Post	1944–48[d] Pre	1944–48[d] Post
Business and professional	33	35	25	18	57	26
White-collar	28	24	22	16	39	21
Skilled and semiskilled	22	19	18	14	23	11
Unskilled	17	15	19	12	23	10
Farmers and farm laborers	23	24	24	16	18	13

a The percentages for the pre-election columns were computed in the same way as the comparable percentages in Table 3.1. The post-election percentages are derived from surveys conducted during the month after the presidential election; they rest, thus, on reported votes in November as compared with the reported vote of four years before.

b The pre-election column rests on a consolidation of AIPO 216T, 217, 218K, 220, 221. The post-election column represents a consolidation of AIPO 224 and 225. Roper's October 1940 survey produced the following D-R percentages: business and professional, 29; white-collar, 26; wage earners, 15; farmers and farm laborers, 15. The occupational categories were not exactly the same as those of the AIPO.

c The pre-election column rests on a consolidation of AIPO 331, 332, 333, 334; the post-election column on AIPO 335 and 336K.

d The pre-election column rests on a consolidation of AIPO 429, 430, and 431; the post-election column on AIPO 432.

acteristics of the data with which we work; it shows switching as measured both by a pre-election expression of preference and by a post-election report of the vote. Except for the election of 1940, a fairly wide difference exists between the two sets of figures. Probably the "true" figures fell somewhere between the two sets of percentages; the data serve better as indicators of contrasting shifts in attitude of groups of voters than as measures of their absolute rates of switching in the voting.[4]

The pattern of recruitment of new voters into the Democratic ranks resembled the patterns of switching among old voters. Democratic losses among old voters decreased from step to step down the ladder of occupational status; the proportion of new voters preferring the Democratic candidate increased from step to step down the ladder. These variations in the voting inclinations of new voters, that is, those who either were too young or simply failed to vote four years earlier, are shown in detail for each of the elections in Table 3.3. A significant

4. Several factors contribute to the differences between the pre-election and post-election findings. The two figures are about alike for 1940, probably the result of the practice in that year of screening many prospective nonvoters from the sample at the interview stage. Beyond that, the pre-election figures rest on a consolidation of several surveys during the campaign, a factor that would tend to overestimate switching since during this era the Democratic vote seemed to reach more complete activation as the campaign progressed. The inclusion of potential nonvoters also probably inflates switching rates; the impression develops that this class of persons has a sharp sensitivity to the winds of the moment and would be especially prone under the circumstances of these campaigns to report a switch in preference. The odds also are that, given the tendency for the popular majority to be inflated in surveys reporting past votes, the post-election surveys understate the actual defection rates. The differences between the pre-election and post-election data for 1948 are especially wide, a factor which lends credence to the supposition that in this campaign quite marked shifts in sentiment occurred in the last ten days or so of the campaign. In this campaign the pre-election polls forecast a Republican victory, much to the glee of the critics of the polls whose forecasts were, incidentally, no better.

TABLE 3.3. Democratic percentage of presidential preference of new voters, within occupational categories, as measured by pre-election and post-election polls[a]

| | 1940 | | 1944 | | 1948 | |
Group	Pre	Post	Pre	Post	Pre	Post
Business and professional	46	42	49	46	39	48
White-collar	53	54	53	66	44	58
Skilled and semiskilled	68	65	59	64	61	75
Unskilled	68	67	63	59	67	69
Farmers and farm laborers	56	48	42	45	48	61

[a] Based on same surveys as Table 3.2. New voters are defined as those who did not vote in the preceding presidential election, either because they were too young or for some other reason.

factor in the maintenance of the position of the "normal" majority probably consists in its success in attracting new voters to its banner. As has been shown (in Table 2.4), the new voters make up a relatively large proportion of the vote, and a failure to capture the loyalties of a majority of them could within a few elections change the balance of power between the parties. Of greatest importance, of course, is the recruitment of young persons who, once they form partisan attachments, may be expected to remain with the party with fair consistency for many years. Yet the older "new voters" are also a numerous, if heterogeneous, category, not without importance in the vote.[5]

5. Over the elections 1940–1960, as shown by Table 2.4, the Democrats drew a somewhat larger proportion of the "new voters" than of the "old" voters, as measured by expressions of pre-election preference. This Democratic advantage in the recruitment of new support doubtless contributed to the maintenance of its position as the party with the larger number of loyal followers. When the new voters at these elections were grouped into age categories, 21–39, 40–59, and 60 and over, the usual pattern over the period was for the Democratic proportion of the pre-election preference to be highest in the 21–39 age group, which suggested uniformly greater Democratic success in recruiting young voters. The notable exception occurred in 1940 when the Democratic

So far our analysis follows conventional forms and yields findings that depend upon our reading into the data plausible assumptions about voter motivation. The data suggest that the issues and alternatives of the time tended to sharpen the class cleavage between the parties and in the process produced voter switching on a scale whose magnitude is not commonly suspected. Yet the analysis also generates persistent doubts. It rests on an assumption that voting can best be understood as an expression of motivations induced by the impact of campaign alternatives on short-range, individual economic interest which we assume to be associated with occupation or status. We impute motives to types of individuals, run the cards through the sorter, and, lo and behold, upper-status persons switch in differing degrees and directions than do lower-status persons. Yet the embarrassing fact remains that in the elections examined many lower-status persons also switched preferences from Democratic to Republican; moreover, many lower-status persons maintained a stand-pat Republican position from election to election. And many well-to-do persons, strange though it may seem, remained steadfast Democrats from election to election.

What would we find if we proceeded directly to motive or attitude and ascertained the relation between vote switching and views on policy? What kinds of relations would be found if we assumed that the voter was a fairly reasonable fellow who voted to promote or to discourage public policies he approved or disapproved, insofar as he could perceive the consequences of his vote? Obviously, all kinds of motives, attitudes, and concerns enter into the voting decision; yet analyses of the available informa-

---

proportion among those 60 and over exceeded the Democratic proportion among those under 40, probably a consequence of the special impact of the old-age security issue on the old folks.

tion indicate quite marked correlations between policy attitudes and vote switching. In short, the data make it appear sensible to regard the voter as a person who is concerned with what governments have done or not done and what they propose to do rather than one guided, perhaps unaware, by the imperatives of economic status or the tricks of Madison Avenue.

Our information on the relation of voter switching to policy preferences is not as comprehensive as we might wish. The information on the election of 1936, which was evidently an event of great significance in the reshaping of the American pattern of party loyalties, is especially limited. Nevertheless, in that year the old-age annuity provisions of the Social Security Act turned out to be a major issue. Republicans attacked the act. All citizens would soon be wearing dog tags carrying their social security numbers and less restrained campaign orators treated the system as a fraud. Voters responded with an expression of opinion startling in its clarity. In the neighborhood of four out of ten 1932 Democratic voters who opposed the legislation shifted over to the Republican candidate while about three out of ten of those 1932 Republicans who favored the plan moved to the support of Roosevelt. The details appear in Table 3.4.* Had the

---

* Editor's note: Key intended to elaborate at some length on the relationship in Table 3.4 between voters' 1936 presidential preference and their attitude toward the old-age insurance program. Attitudes on the social security issue may have had two broad effects on the 1936 voting. In addition to making voters whose position on the issue was not congruent with their previous presidential vote more likely to switch parties in 1936, it also may have made individuals whose previous presidential vote and policy attitude on the social security question were mutually consistent more inclined to stick with the party they had previously supported. Among 1932 Democratic voters, although four in ten of those who opposed the old-age insurance plan switched to the G.O.P. in 1936, only one in eight of the 1932 Democrats who supported federal old-age pensions left the Democratic party at the next presidential elec-

social security issue been the only influence on the vote
these switches would have been closer to ten out of ten
in each direction. It was not, of course, the only issue.*
Nevertheless, an impressive relation between voting behavior and policy preference on this question prevailed,
which raises a presumption that the social security issue
had a notable power to wrench voters from their 1932
party positions to a vote in accord with their policy preferences.

As the election of 1940 approached, newspaper headlines tended to focus on the threat of war; yet voters
seemed to be more concerned with the grand issues of
domestic politics. Those issues turned broadly around the
place and power of business in the American system, and
the Democratic Administration occupied the role, in the
eyes of business, as the enemy of business and, in the
eyes of others, as the protagonist of the generality. The
tolerant attitude of government toward the sitdown
strikes in the automobile industry in 1937 symbolized the
situation. As the 1940 polling neared, however, business
protests became sharper as earlier New Deal legislation,

---

tion. On the other hand, 1932 Republican voters who supported the
insurance plan were much more likely to switch to the Democratic presidential nominee in 1936 than were 1932 Republican voters who opposed the Social Security pension plan. Three in ten of the 1932 Republican voters who supported the plan switched to Roosevelt in 1936;
only 7 per cent of the 1932 Republican voters who opposed the plan
deserted the G.O.P. in 1936.

* Editor's note: The data in Table 3.4 do not indicate how important
or visible the social security issue was to the members of Dr. Gallup's
sample. Some voters, for example, may have duly registered their approval or disapproval of the old-age insurance scheme without really
caring very much about its inclusion in the Social Security Act; and
Key intended to emphasize that undoubtedly the social security issue
was more salient for some voters than for others during the 1936 campaign. Either a lack of concern over the social security question or a
greater concern with other issues among some voters could help explain
why the relation between policy attitudes on social security and 1936
voting behavior was not even stronger than it was.

made temporarily ineffective by constitutional litigation, began to make its effects felt. The defeat of Roosevelt's plan for the rejuvenation of the Supreme Court heartened business only temporarily. The Court found ways and means to hold major New Deal legislation constitutional, contrary to the opinions of most of the corporation lawyers in the country. Employers, thus, began to feel the bite of the Wagner Labor Relations Act. Wendell Willkie, an erstwhile Democrat and former president of a utility corporation that had had to sell out to the Tennessee Valley Authority, won the Republican nomination and led the forces of protest against the New Deal.

How did the voters respond to the campaign alternatives? Did their response proceed from their preferences about governmental policy? Or did voters react in a random fashion as the winds of the campaign blew them

TABLE 3.4. Switches in presidential voting preference, 1932–1936, in relation to response to question: "Do you favor the compulsory old-age insurance plan, starting January first, which requires employers and employees to make equal monthly contributions?"[a]

Response	% of 1932 D's, D-R	% of 1932 R's, R-D	% of new voters, D[b]
Yes, favor	12 (1,630)	30 (643)	61 (626)
No	40 (483)	7 (535)	45 (245)
No opinion	13 (315)	16 (175)	71 (170)

[a] AIPO 53, 9-26-36. This is the only surviving deck of cards for a 1936 survey with a recall of the 1932 vote. Data on the characteristics of the sample are nonexistent, but the addition of the N's to produce a national sample would probably be even more perilous than is the use here made of the data. The N's appear in parentheses. As in Table 2.1 and other tables, N is the total number of respondents on which the percentage is based. Thus, the figure 1,630 in the first column means that there were 1,630 respondents who recalled having voted for the Democratic candidate in 1932 and who favored the compulsory old-age insurance plan in 1936. Of these 1,630 persons, 12 per cent reported that they intended to support the Republican candidate in 1936.

[b] New voters are respondents who had not voted in 1932, either because they were too young or for other reasons.

about? To an astonishing degree (that is, a degree astonishing to persons with experience in the analysis of polling
data) voters in their movements to and fro across party
lines and from an inactive to an active voting status be-
haved as persons who made choices congruent with their
policy preferences. In a sense, the question of more or less
government control of business bundled up most of the
lesser domestic questions of the campaign into a single
great issue. Of those 1936 Democratic voters who felt that
there should be less government regulation of business,
about half expressed an intent to defect to Willkie in 1940.
Of the 1936 Republican voters who thought there should
be less business regulation, 98 per cent remained steadfastly Republican (and the 2 per cent desertion to the
Democrats is not in excess of error that could have been
produced in recording interviews and in processing the
data). Few 1936 Republican voters favored the existing
level of business regulation or more regulation, but those
who did succumbed far more frequently to Democratic
blandishments; about 15 per cent of them favored Roosevelt. Table 3.5 contains the details.[6]

An even more marked association prevailed between

6. For the nontechnical reader, it should be explained that the probability of divergence between the sample percentages in the tables and
the true percentages in the sampled population is higher with small
samples. Hence, the fact that a poll estimates fairly closely the percentage division of the two-party vote of the nation does not mean that
percentages for subdivisions of the sample, for instance, Negroes or
unskilled workers, are equally near the true percentages. The chances
are high for greater sampling divergencies, on both the high and low
sides, for subsamples. Further, the technicians judge that recent polls
are superior to earlier ones in their sampling techniques, in their
interviewing practices, and in their administration. For the technician,
it should be said that the N's of the tables cannot usually be added
to produce the total N of a specific survey or combination of surveys;
no attempt has been made to account for all the miscellaneous categories of respondents not relevant to our main purpose. The N's may
be used, though, to compare the size of the various cells as defined.

TABLE 3.5. Switches in presidential voting preference, 1936–1940, in relation to response to question: "During the next four years do you think there should be more or less regulation of business by the Federal government than at present?"[a]

Response	% of 1936 D's, D-R	% of 1936 R's, R-D	% of new voters, D[b]
More regulation	10 (856)[c]	15 (161)	73 (187)
About same	10 (712)	16 (122)	76 (124)
Less regulation	50 (841)	2 (1,263)	32 (229)
No opinion	14 (637)	8 (158)	68 (148)

[a] A consolidation of AIPO 215K-T, 10-9-40, and 219K-T, 10-24-40.

[b] New voters consist of those respondents who had not voted in 1936 either because they were too young or for other reasons.

[c] Here is an illustration of how to read the table entries: these two figures mean that, of the 856 poll respondents in 1940 who said they had voted for Roosevelt in 1936 and who wanted more regulation in the 1940's, 10 per cent expressed an intent to defect to Willkie.

voter attitudes on farm policy and shifts across party lines. About seven out of ten Democrats of 1936 who became disillusioned about the farm program had a 1940 preference for Willkie. Republican defectors were not numerous but about one out of five 1936 Republicans who approved the Democratic farm program looked favorably on Roosevelt in 1940. Those with the appropriate policy outlooks stood pat in remarkable degree. Only 1 per cent of the 1936 Republicans who disapproved the Administration farm program threatened to vote Democratic. This relationship between policy outlook and vote (shown in detail in Table 3.6) doubtless reflected to a degree the tendency of a voter on a specific question to improvise policy views that seem to be consistent with the way he planned to vote for other reasons entirely. A steadfast Democratic partisan might have been expected to opine that the "Roosevelt administration has done a good job in handling the farm problem," if the question were put to him in that form. Yet, however such opinions come into being, their supportive function in the political system should be the same.

By 1940 the Supreme Court had held the Wagner Labor Relations Act constitutional; nevertheless, many employers remained hopeful of the ultimate repeal or modification of the act. The only way to fulfill that hope was to defeat Roosevelt. The electorate responded predictably to the impact of the issue. Of the 1936 Democrats who had come to believe that the act should be repealed (which, in the context of the times, was an antilabor move) about one out of two expressed a 1940 Republican preference. Those who thought it should merely be revised defected only about half as frequently. Similarly, Republican loyalties were maintained most steadfastly by those who stood for repeal or revision of the act. Interestingly, in our sample of 1936 nonvoters only nine respondents turned up favoring the repeal of the act; eight of the nine pre-

TABLE 3.6. Switches in presidential voting preference, 1936–1940, in relation to views on Roosevelt Administration's program for helping farmers[a]

View	% of 1936 D's, D-R	% of 1936 R's, R-D	% of new voters, D
Approve[b]	7 (978)	23 (131)	83 (242)
Disapprove	69 (202)	1 (529)	16 (134)
No opinion	22 (269)	6 (170)	60 (130)

[a] AIPO 215K&T, 10-9-40.

[b] In this survey the schedule was split and the question was put in a slightly different form in the K and T versions. One question form was: "Do you think the Roosevelt administration has done a good job, or a poor job, in handling the farm problem in this country?" The other was: "In general do you approve or disapprove of the Roosevelt administration's program for helping farmers?" The "approve" version drew 50 per cent approval; the "good" version found only 42 per cent who thought the administration had done a good job. The two surveys are consolidated in this analysis.

ferred Willkie. Withal, vote switches occurred in directions consistent with the assumption that voters were moved by a rational calculation of the instrumental impact of their vote. The detailed data are in Table 3.7.[7]

TABLE 3.7. Switches in presidential voting preference, 1936–1940, in relation to response to question: "Do you think the Wagner Labor Act should be revised, repealed or left unchanged?"[a]

Response	% of 1936 D's, D-R	% of 1936 R's, R-D	% of new voters, D
Revised	24 (193)	3 (258)	59 (90)
Repealed	52 (42)	3 (77)	b
Left unchanged	12 (376)	12 (91)	64 (106)
No opinion	22 (497)	5 (283)	59 (192)

[a] AIPO 215K&T, 10-9-40. The analysis is limited to those who said they had "heard of" the Wagner Act.

[b] Only 9 respondents fell in this cell; one reported a Democratic preference.

Roosevelt's candidacy in 1940 ran counter to the two-term tradition, a fact that agitated the citizenry, especially those who opposed him on other grounds anyway. And probably those who supported him on other grounds declined in an especial degree to become exercised about the third-term question. In any case, the great shifts of the electorate had a close relationship to attitude on the third-term question, as may be seen from Table 3.8. Of the 1936 Democrats who felt that under no condition should a President serve three terms, nearly 90 per cent moved over to a Republican preference in 1940. On the

7. The labor issue had begun to take its toll of 1936 Democratic voters by the time of the congressional election of 1938. A survey during the congressional campaign asked: "Do you think the National Labor Relations Board is fair to businessmen and other employers?" Among 1936 Democratic presidential voters who thought the board unfair, 31 per cent favored Republican congressional candidates; among those who thought it fair, only 14 per cent did so. AIPO 135, 10-8-38.

other hand, 1936 Republicans who became 1940 Democrats tended to hold moderate views on the third-term matter. They could see the necessity for exceptions. These relations do not, of course, establish that persons opposed to a third term in principle defected from the Democracy for that reason. An alternative assumption is that they adopted that position because they chose to defect from the Democracy. Whatever its origin, the congruence of outlook on the constitutional issue and the direction of the vote is of importance, and it is not unreasonable to suppose that a goodly number of persons may very well have been governed in their candidate choice by their policy outlook.

The opinion surveys during the campaigns of 1944 and of 1948 included few inquiries suitable for the identification of policy-related movements of voters in those elections. From the behavior of persons of different economic

TABLE 3.8. Switches in presidential voting preference, 1936–1940, in relation to views on third-term question[a]

Views	% of 1936 D's, D-R		% of 1936 R's, R-D		% of new voters, D	
Silly and outworn tradition	5	(521)	14	(56)	83	(98)
Not good, but exceptions	8	(1,390)	20	(243)	15	(369)
Under no condition	88	(332)	0.3	(989)	5	(189)
Don't know	15	(59)	4	(23)	68	(28)

[a] Based on Roper survey, October 1940. The question was:

"With which one of these statements concerning a third term do you come closest to agreeing?

"a) The idea that a President should not hold office for three terms is a silly and outworn tradition.

"b) While it may not generally be a good idea for a President to serve three terms, there should be no rule at a time of national crisis.

"c) Never under any conditions should a President hold office for three terms."

and occupational status (presented earlier in Tables 3.1 and 3.2) it is a fair assumption that patterns quite similar to those of 1940 prevailed in 1948 and probably to a lesser extent in 1944 when war muted to some extent the divisive issues of domestic policy.[8] One relevant analysis from the 1948 election appears in Table 3.9, which presents our

TABLE 3.9. Switches in presidential vote, 1944–1948, in relation to response to question: "As things stand today, do you think the laws governing labor unions are too strict or not strict enough?"[a]

Response	% of 1944 D's, D-R	% of 1944 R's, R-D	% of new voters, D
Too strict	8 (304)	22 (76)	74 (80)
About right	15 (357)	9 (218)	68 (118)
Not strict enough	27 (232)	6 (318)	51 (87)
No opinion	15 (181)	10 (101)	64 (58)

[a] Based on AIPO 432, 11-1-48. Interviews were conducted after the election; the date is the "send-out" date.

familiar pattern of switching in its relation to views on the question whether the laws governing labor unions were too strict or not strict enough. By 1948 the Wagner Act had been revised by the Taft-Hartley Act to the disadvantage of unions. The AFL and CIO exerted themselves in support of Harry S. Truman who urged repeal of the act, a position which by now had become a prolabor position. The evidence from this question supports the conventional view that the campaign of 1948 shaped antagonisms along New Deal and anti-New Deal lines.

8. Unhappiness with wartime economic controls doubtless contributed to Democratic defections in 1944. In a 1944 survey the following question was put: "After the war in Europe is over, should the following government controls be continued or discontinued? a) Food rationing? b) Gasoline rationing? c) Price ceilings on things people buy?" The D-R percentages among "continued" and "discontinued" groups of 1940 Democratic voters were: a) 15 and 20; b) 12 and 21; c) 16 and 21. AIPO 331, 10-6-44.

Those few Dewey supporters of 1944 who felt that labor laws were too strict deserted to Truman at a rate of about one out of five in 1948. On the other hand, 1944 Roosevelt supporters who thought the labor laws not strict enough switched to Dewey with somewhat higher frequency, as the table indicates.

As the campaign of 1940 approached, the threat of war preoccupied the pundits and the commentators, who doubtless communicated their anxieties to the public. Yet the promises made and expectations raised by the candidates with respect to foreign policy seemed to have far less bearing on the vote than did questions of domestic policy. For a time foreign policy seemed to have been taken out of the campaign, but as the election neared, Willkie, under the prodding of the Republican professionals, stirred up the issue by his forecasts that war would soon come if Roosevelt were re-elected. Democratic campaigners probably became more worried about these charges than did the electorate generally.[9] At any rate, the data indicate a comparatively mild relation between attitudes on foreign policy and vote shifting.

The question whether it was more important to keep out of war ourselves or to help England even at the risk of getting into war should have separated persons into the two conflicting camps of the time. Though more of those who thought that we should keep out of war deserted to Willkie, the difference between this figure and the rate of desertion of those who thought we should help England win (Table 3.10) was not wide enough to indicate that this difference in attitude contributed nearly so heavily to vote switching as did the impact of domestic issues. Similarly, a person's views on the question whether we should have gotten into World War I might be expected

9. On this aspect of the 1940 campaign, see R. E. Sherwood, *Roosevelt and Hopkins* (New York: Bantam, 1950), ch. 8.

TABLE 3.10. Switches in presidential voting preference, 1936–1940, in relation to opinions on whether more important to keep out of war or to help England win[a]

Attitude	% of 1936 D's, D-R	% of 1936 R's, R-D	% of new voters, D
Keep out of war	31 (1,975)	3 (1,127)	56 (724)
Help England win	19 (2,426)	5 (1,211)	61 (653)
No choice	25 (166)	0 (76)	72 (68)

[a] A consolidation of AIPO 217, 10-22-40; 220, 10-22-40; 224, 11-19-40. Note that a post-election survey is combined with two pre-election surveys. The question was: "Which of these two things do you think is the more important for the United States to try to do: 1. To keep out of war ourselves, 2. To help England win, even at the risk of getting into war." The schedules carried the "no choice" box, though the meaning of this response is unclear.

to segregate those of isolationist sentiment from their opponents. Those 1936 Democrats who thought our World War I venture was a mistake shifted to Willkie more frequently than did those who held an opposing view; yet again the difference (Table 3.11) was relatively small.

This is not to say that foreign policy questions invariably command less attention than do domestic questions. Rather in 1940 this seemed to be the case. Probably the more general rule is that the electorate responds most markedly and most clearly to those events it has experienced and observed, vicariously or directly. Voters

TABLE 3.11. Switches in presidential vote, 1936–1940, in relation to response to question: "Do you think it was a mistake for the United States to enter the last World War?"[a]

Response	% of 1936 D's, D-R	% of 1936 R's, R-D	% of new voters, D
Yes, mistake	28 (511)	4 (382)	49 (140)
No	18 (636)	5 (322)	64 (154)
No opinion	20 (258)	6 (118)	67 (108)

[a] AIPO 224, 11-19-40.

had enjoyed or not enjoyed eight years of domestic policy of the New Deal and they reacted demonstrably to those experiences. The prospects for the future may generally tend less to engage the voter or to govern his actions. Those prospects tend to be hazy, uncertain, problematic. Voters may respond most assuredly to what they have seen, heard, experienced. Forecasts, promises, predicted disaster, or pie in the sky may be less moving.

A kind word needs to be said for that supposedly benighted fellow, the standpatter, the consistent party voter. So far our attention has centered on the switcher. The evidence indicates that the shifting voter is far more numerous than is commonly supposed. Moreover, his reports of his actions and attitudes indicate that as he navigates his way from party to party he moves in a manner that is sensible in the light of his policy preferences. To be sure, partisan loyalties invest the electoral mass with a degree of inertia and not all voters follow their policy inclinations by moving from candidate to candidate.[10] What of these voters who remain in the party ranks from election to election? Are they obtuse diehards who swallow their principles to stick by their party?

Almost all the analyses of the preceding pages throw light on the question. On issue after issue those with views consistent with the outlook of their party stood pat in their voting preference. Notably few Republican defections occurred among those who subscribed to sound

10. The data used in this study permit no analyses to ascertain the relation between consistent party support and the sense of party identification which has been extensively examined by Angus Campbell and his associates of the Survey Research Center of the University of Michigan. Doubtless the standpatters of our tables who resist the pull of their policy inclinations toward the opposite party include large numbers of "strong" party identifiers, that is, persons who regard themselves as "strong" Republicans or Democrats in their responses to interviewers of the Survey Research Center.

Republican doctrine. Democratic deserters were uniformly fewest among those who concurred with the pure and orthodox Democratic tenets of the time. No doubt some Republicans and some Democrats adjusted their views to make them conform with their perceptions of the positions of their party. Yet it is the parallelism of vote and policy view that is significant for our analysis, not its origin.

The facts seem to be that, on the average, the stand-patters do not have to behave as mugwumps to keep their consciences clear; they are already where they ought to be in the light of their policy attitudes. Tables 3.12, 3.13, and 3.14 demonstrate this point in another way.* Those who vote consistently from one election to the next, the data of those tables indicate, adhere to the party doctrine in high degree. Though partisan groupings of voters are not models of ideological purity, the standpatters of each party manifest fairly high agreement with the party positions as popularly perceived. Thus, well over half of the 1936–1940 D-D's felt that there should be during the next four years about the same degree or more government regulation. Similarly, the Administration's farm program found favor with three fourths of the 1936–1940 D-D's, while only a little more than 10 per cent of the R-R's could bring themselves to approve it. Again far fewer of the

---

* Editor's note: At this point Key planned to comment further on Tables 3.12, 3.13, and 3.14, and to stress how they differ from Table 3.11 and some of the other tables presented earlier in this chapter. These earlier tables focused attention on the percentages of persons interviewed who switched parties between two consecutive elections and the presidential preferences of new voters in relation to their position on specified policy questions. The earlier tables emphasized the policy preferences of voters who switched parties from one election to the next. Tables 3.12, 3.13, and 3.14 present data for all voters in each major party camp—new voters, standpatters, and switchers. They indicate the distribution of given policy preferences among each group of voters. Data presented in this form highlight the degree to which the standpatters tend to endorse doctrinal positions usually associated with the party they support.

TABLE 3.12. Pattern of presidential preference, 1936–1940, in relation to distribution of responses to question: "During the next four years do you think there should be more or less regulation of business by the Federal government than at present?"[a]

Response	D-D	R-D	0-D[b]	0-R[b]	D-R	R-R
More regulation	32%	28%	34%	18%	13%	8%
About same	27	23	23	10	11	7
Less regulation	18	34	18	55	63	76
No opinion	23	15	25	17	13	9
	100	100	100	100	100	100
N[c]	(2,386)	(85)	(403)	(285)	(660)	(1,619)

[a] A consolidation of AIPO 215K-T, 10-9-40, and 219K-T, 10-24-40 (as in Table 3.5).

[b] New voters, i.e., nonvoters in 1936.

[c] As in all tables, the figures in parentheses, technically known as N, are the numbers of survey respondents on which the percentages are based. For example, 2,386 of those interviewed were Democratic standpatters (according to their replies) and 1,619 were Republican standpatters. Of these 1,619, only 8 per cent wanted more regulation of business.

TABLE 3.13. Patterns of presidential preference, 1936–1940, in relation to distribution of views on Roosevelt Administration's program for handling farm problem[a]

Response	D-D	R-D	0-D[b]	0-R[b]	D-R	R-R
Approve	76%	64%	66%	19%	26%	13%
Disapprove	5	13	7	55	51	66
Don't know	18	21	26	25	22	20
No answer	1	2	1	1	1	1
	100	100	100	100	100	100
N	(1,191)	(47)	(305)	(207)	(274)	(795)

[a] Based on AIPO 215K&T, 10-9-40, as in Table 3.6, which see for the form of the question.

[b] Nonvoters in 1936.

TABLE 3.14. Patterns of presidential preference, 1944–1948, in relation to distribution of responses to question: "As things stand today, do you think the laws governing labor unions are too strict or not strict enough?"[a]

Response	D-D	R-D	0-D	0-R	D-R	R-R
Too strict	31%	26%	27%	17%	15%	9%
About right	33	31	36	31	31	31
Not strict enough	19	28	20	35	38	46
No opinion	17	15	17	17	16	14
	100	100	100	100	100	100
N	(909)	(65)	(220)	(123)	(165)	(648)

[a] Based on AIPO 432, 11-1-48, a post-election survey (interviews were conducted after the election; the date is the "send-out" date).

1944–1948 D-D's than of the 1944–1948 R-R's thought that the laws governing labor unions were too strict.[11]

Party switchers move towards the party whose stand-patters they resemble in their policy views, a proposition made apparent by the tables. The D-R's are divided in their policy views in about the same fashion as the R-R's with whom they join in the election, and the R-D's resemble the D-D's to which they attach themselves for the voting. The nonvoters at the preceding election who join the D-D's or the R-R's also have an attitudinal resemblance to the standpatters with whom they ally them-

11. Standpatters, the evidence suggests, acquire their policy attitudes in at least two ways. Some persons more or less deliberately affiliate with the party whose policy emphases appear to parallel their own. Other persons, psychologically identified with a party, adopt those policy outlooks espoused by the more prominent spokesmen of their party. In the course of party life, the acceptance of the cues of party leadership may result in alteration of the attitudes of party followers. This flexible conformity with shifting party doctrine probably occurs most markedly among those strongly identified psychologically with the party. See Angus Campbell and Homer C. Cooper, *Group Differences in Attitudes and Votes* (Ann Arbor: Survey Research Center, 1956), pp. 102-104.

selves. Yet, as the tables also indicate, the switchers bear earmarks of their origin. The D-R's are not in quite the same degree as the R-R's attached to the party policy position, and the R-D's also bore traces of their Republican origin. Nevertheless, on balance each of these groups bore far greater resemblance to the standpatters of the party of their destination than to the faithful of the party of their origin.

One major problem remains to be touched on, if not disposed of. That is the problem of the role of personality in the maintenance of the Democratic following during the 1930's and 1940's. How do we cope with the assertion that the series of Democratic victories reflected the massive appeal of the personality of Franklin Delano Roosevelt and nothing more? Even the most cursory reflection destroys this type of explanation in its crude form. It becomes ridiculous immediately if one contemplates what the fate of Franklin Delano Roosevelt would have been had he from 1933 to 1936 stood for those policies which were urged upon the country by the reactionaries of the day. Before 1932 acute political observers had seen him as only a pleasant country gentleman of the Hudson Valley who had a yearning to be president. He became, though, a formidable and wicked opponent to his enemies and a savior to those who regarded him as their champion. His position derived not so much from the kind of a man he was as from the kinds of things for which, and against which, he fought. His personal qualities may have intensified both hatred and love for him. And the popular image of Roosevelt doubtless enabled many persons to support and to oppose him without detailed knowledge of what policies he was for or against; they could accurately regard him as for or against their kind of people.

Neither our data nor the analytical tools of social science permit completely satisfactory appraisals of the place of personality in the determination of the vote. Nevertheless, some wisps of evidence—more or less tautological in nature—have a relevance to the question. In 1940 Dr. Gallup's interviewers asked the respondents in his sample: "If the United States should get into the war, which man would you prefer to have as President—Roosevelt or Willkie?" To ask such a question might be thought to be about the same as to ask, "For whom, as of today, do you plan to vote?" Yet the question raised a perfectly legitimate problem, one to which the citizen should address himself if he is to perform his classical role of recording relevant and responsible decisions as he votes. What did the response to the vote indicate? Some, but not many, 1936 Landon voters opined that Roosevelt would, indeed, be the better man if we got into war, and about half of them, probably reluctantly, had decided to defect from the Republican ranks to support Roosevelt. On the other hand, a goodly number of 1936 Democratic voters liked what they saw in Willkie as a potential wartime leader; 97 per cent of them moved to the Republican side, as Willkie himself had done only a short time before. For the details see Table 3.15.

In 1944 the National Opinion Research Center put questions to a national sample which showed somewhat similar patterns of voter movement. At the time of this campaign one popular concern was the successful conclusion of World War II; moreover, some people were beginning to worry about the shape of public policy when peace came again. The NORC asked in October 1944: "Sometimes one man does a better job of handling certain problems than another man. Do you think Roosevelt or Dewey would do a better job of winning the war?" A very

TABLE 3.15. Switches in presidential voting preference, 1936–1940, in relation to response to question: "If the U.S. should get into the war, which man would you prefer to have as President—Roosevelt or Willkie?"[a]

Response	% of 1936 D's, D-R	% of 1936 R's, R-D	% of new voters, D
Roosevelt	4 (1,158)	47 (59)	93 (341)
Willkie	97 (329)	[b] (717)	4 (157)
Undecided	52 (71)	0 (54)	45 (44)

[a] Based on AIPO 220, 10-22-40.

[b] Less than one half of 1 per cent; one respondent in this cell reported a shift to Roosevelt.

few 1940 Democrats had arrived at the conclusion that Dewey could do a better job of winding up hostilities; most of them switched to Republican in 1944. A much larger number of Willkie voters of 1940 felt obliged to concede that Roosevelt was a better man for this particular job. About a third of them had decided to vote for him, while their fellow Republicans who saw merit in Mr. Dewey stood almost to a man with the G.O.P. The exact figures appear in Table 3.16. The same survey put a question on whether Dewey or Roosevelt would do better at "providing jobs after the war." The familiar movements and countermovements in consonance with voter judgments on this issue occurred, as Table 3.17 indicates.

For those who have persevered to this point, a few preliminary reflections on the significance of the information so far assembled are in order. We have established patterns of movement of party switchers from election to election and the patterns of stability of the standpatter that lead us to a conception of the voter that is not often propounded. From our analyses the voter emerges as a person who appraises the actions of government, who has

TABLE 3.16. Switches in presidential voting preference, 1940–1944, in relation to response to question: "Sometimes one man does a better job of handling certain problems than another man. Do you think Roosevelt or Dewey would do a better job of winning the war?"[a]

Response	% of 1940 D's, D-R	% of 1940 R's, R-D	% of new voters, D
Roosevelt	6 (828)	35 (114)	87 (144)
Dewey	90 (29)	0 (257)	3 (29)
No difference	44 (100)	3 (335)	12 (48)
Don't know	45 (29)	0 (56)	21 (14)

[a] NORC 30/229, October 1944.

policy preferences, and who relates his vote to those appraisals and preferences. One may have misgivings about the data and one can certainly concede that the data also indicate that some voters are governed by blind party loyalty and that some others respond automatically to the winds of the environment of the moment. Yet the obtrusive feature of the data is the large number of persons whose vote is instrumental to their policy preferences.

These parallelisms of voting patterns and policy prefer-

TABLE 3.17. Switches in presidential voting preference, 1940–1944, in relation to response to question: "Sometimes one man does a better job of handling certain problems than another man. Do you think Roosevelt or Dewey would do a better job of providing jobs after the war?"[a]

Response	% of 1940 D's, D-R	% of 1940 R's, R-D	% of new voters, D
Roosevelt	3 (747)	52 (63)	93 (124)
Dewey	82 (88)	1 (556)	1 (69)
No difference	25 (73)	12 (92)	42 (19)
Don't know	24 (74)	2 (49)	41 (22)

[a] NORC 30/229, October 1944.

ences may be dismissed as the meaningless result of the disposition of people to adopt consistent sets of views on interrelated matters. A survey respondent, bedeviled by an interviewer, may express a preference for a Democratic candidate and then, to keep things tidy, adopt a favorable attitude toward Democratic policy positions. He would, though, in our analysis fit into the same pigeonhole of the IBM sorter as the person who arrived at the same consistent constellation of attitudes by a process of anguished thought and reflection. Doubtless both kinds of respondents are encountered by poll interviewers. Yet, however these patterns of consistent voting preferences are formed, they can scarcely be regarded as without political significance. Our correlations, though, should not be taken to mean that the policy attitudes correlated with changes and continuities in voting preference necessarily cause those changes or continuities. Rather they demonstrate the tendency of persons to build up combinations of outlooks and to adopt voting preferences that make sense in the light of those outlooks.

In another direction our data throw light on the interactions between government and public and on the functions of the electorate in the democratic process. A notable element of our tables is the extent to which an Administration seems to lose the votes of its erstwhile supporters who dissent from actions it has taken. The tables seem to verify the journalistic superstition that the people only vote against; never, for. That appearance results in part from the manner in which the facts have been presented; an equally strong case could be made for the proposition that the standpatters stand pat because they are for what has been done. Nevertheless, the fact remains that some erstwhile supporters do vote against and they tend to disagree with actions that have been taken. Few erstwhile enemies are attracted to a dominant party by its actions, though some are. A president may, with justification, be anxious lest a projected action draw down his reservoir of popular good will. He cannot proceed on the assumption that inaction will maintain the loyalty of the faithful by antagonizing no one. Yet to govern he must be prepared to expend some of his good will. And to continue to govern he must attempt to offset those losses by policies that attract support from the opposition or from among the new voters.*

The patterns of flow of the major streams of shifting voters graphically reflect the electorate in its great, and perhaps principal, role as an appraiser of past events, past performance, and past actions. It judges retrospectively; it commands prospectively only insofar as it expresses either approval or disapproval of that which has happened before. Voters may reject what they have known; or they may approve what they have known. They are not likely to be attracted in great numbers by promises of the novel or unknown. Once innovation has occurred they may embrace it, even though they would have, earlier, hesitated to venture forth to welcome it.

These tendencies of the electorate, as they obtrude from our many tables, make plain how completely the minority party is a captive of the majority—and of the situation. Critics of the American party system fret because the minority party does not play the role of an imaginative advocate heralding the shape of a new world. In truth, it gains votes most notably from among those groups who are disappointed by, who disapprove of, or who regard

* Editor's note: At this point Key intended to elaborate on this "maintenance process"—stressing both the importance to the governing party of maintaining the loyalty of its previous supporters and its need to win converts from the opposition and additional new support among the new voters.

themselves as injured by, the actions of the Administration. The opposition can maximize its strength as it centers its fire on those elements of the Administration program disliked by the largest numbers of people. Thus, as a matter of practical politics, it must appear to be a common scold rather than a bold exponent of innovation, though it may propose new (or old) approaches to old questions. The misfortunes of the Republicans over the period 1932–1952 sprang essentially from the simple fact that they could not lay their hands on an issue on which the Democrats had outraged enough people to vote them out of office.

CHAPTER 4

REPUBLICAN INTERLUDE

The election of 1952 may severely test our hypothesis that voters, or at least many of them, are sensible persons who vote in a manner calculated to nudge public affairs in the direction they judge desirable. That election, a goodly number of stalwart Democrats and some critics of the democratic process believe, demonstrated that a well-financed party amply staffed with cunning propaganda specialists can humbug a majority of the voters. Zealous supporters of Eisenhower took another view: they regarded the election as a triumph of virtue against wicked odds. Yet even Madison Avenue winced as it received credit for psychological tricks that were supposed to have carried the day for a business community arrayed behind an attractive but compliant front. A simpler explanation may be closer to the truth; the simpler explanation may always be closer to the truth. What of the evidence for another possibility? What if we should suppose that the electorate looked at the public scene, did not like what it saw, and performed that act of governance for which an electorate is superbly equipped, that is, it threw the ins out?

The campaign of 1952 found the American people preoccupied with more than their normal quota of anxieties, frustrations, and concerns. The successful conclusion of World War II, at great cost and some sacrifice, had, it seemed, really concluded nothing. The termination of hostilities had only inaugurated an endless era of internal tension and friction. Our erstwhile ally, Soviet Russia, had become our enemy, and Communism's advances in every corner of the world destroyed whatever remained of the American dream of a domestic serenity undisturbed by the woes of the rest of the globe. With American aid, what was left of Europe was rearming itself to block Soviet expansion from the East. In the Far East China had fallen to the Communists who proceeded to move into Indo-China and Tibet. In 1950 came the challenge that finally provoked a response. North Koreans, provisioned and trained by the Communist regimes of China and Russia, invaded South Korea. The defense, formally under United Nations auspices, fell principally to the United States. And the Korean War did not appear to go well for us. A disinclination to take steps that might lead to a full-fledged war with China generated unease in a people that traditionally had regarded wars as events that sooner or later came to an unmistakable conclusion—followed in due course by pensions for the participants.

According to some of the demonologists of the day, our vicissitudes abroad could be explained by wrongheadedness, if not by treachery, at home. China, thus, fell to Communism, not because of the strength of Communist forces and the rottenness of the old regime, but because of lapses in the State Department. In 1950 Senator Joseph McCarthy initiated his series of strident charges and heavy-handed investigations. From other, and more reliable, sources revelations and charges of espionage lent a color of credibility to, though they did not establish, the assertion that Russia had developed the atom bomb so quickly because of the excellence of her spy system rather than the skill of her scientists. As such charges crowded the headlines day after day, the Korean episode wore on to be punctuated by a constitutional crisis in 1951 when President Truman relieved General Douglas MacArthur of his Korean command because of insubordination, no more, no less, yet insubordination of a sort not perceived as such by all hands. The General came home to fade away and fade away he did but not without reinforcing the impression held by many that the management of the Republic was erratic.

Petty scandals in government did not improve the appearance of the Administration. Investigations followed by indictments and resignations gave indication of a relaxed administration of the tax laws, though President Truman responded with a successful drive to replace politically appointed district collectors of internal revenue with government career men, a considerable achievement by any standard. Critics of the Administration got political mileage from investigations of the Reconstruction Finance Corporation and its relations with White House staffers. The untimely acquisition of a mink coat by the wife of one official and the gift of a deep freeze to another official translated complex situations into "mink coats" and "deep freezes," symbols of wide comprehensibility within the population. And anti-Administration propagandists tried to make something of poker-playing and the consumption of bourbon in the White House—and perhaps they succeeded at least with some people.

Republican platform drafters, in the traditional manner of platform drafters, indulged in strong language as they characterized the Democratic Administration. "We charge that they have plunged us into war in Korea without the consent of our citizens through their authorized representatives in the Congress, and have carried on that war without will to victory." With even less restraint, the platform charged that "They have shielded traitors to the Nation in high places." The platform asserted that "there has been corruption in high places," to the shame of the moral standards of the American people. The foundations of the Republic had been so undermined "as to threaten its existence." The rhetoricians gloomily and at length analyzed the state of the country, and pointed to the road to peace and solvency under Republican auspices. But the emphasis was on the attack: "Communism, Corruption, Korea."

History will deal far more kindly with the Truman Administration than did the Republican platform of 1952. Of the far-reaching significance of President Truman's great innovations in foreign policy, there can be no doubt. Of the importance for the free world of the quick response to the attack on South Korea, there can be little reservation. The object at the moment, though, is not to appraise —or to praise—the accomplishments of his Administration. Nor is it to guess whether a different Administration could have had sufficient foresight, political skill, power, or wisdom to have prevented those events in which things indubitably went sour. The object is rather to convey a suggestion of the style and content of the picture of the political world that predominated in the communications flow of the time, for our purpose is to examine the responses of the voters to the situation they saw. The grand outlines of their response were, of course, obvious enough. A sharp upward trend in political interest brought nearly 12 million more voters to the polls than had the election of 1948. Of the major-party voters, 55.4 per cent supported the Republican candidate, General Dwight D.

Eisenhower. The simplest explanation of the episode is that the voters used the only real weapon possessed by the people in a popular regime. They ousted from power a political party of whose performance they disapproved. But what of the evidence for so disarming an explanation? What attitudes did voters hold that may make the assertion plausible or implausible?

From a conventional analysis, the election of 1952 appears to have been the final stage in the ebbing away of the overwhelming majority amassed by the New Deal in 1936. The Democratic proportion of the presidential vote sagged a few points at each election after its extraordinary peak in 1936. From one election to the next, as our earlier Table 3.1 indicated, Democrats of all status levels defected to the Republicans, though the defection rate tended to be higher among upper-status Democrats. This same sort of seepage, apparently with less class bias, continued from 1948 to 1952 on a scale sufficient to move the Democratic vote down below the winning level. The movements, from Democratic to Republican and vice versa, from 1948 to 1952 are shown for a variety of categories of voters by Table 4.1.

By 1952, too, a creeping moderation had affected the pattern of partisan cleavages. The vote of that year less nearly approximated a split along occupational or status lines than had the cleavages of the piping days of the New Deal. Class tensions, generated by the conditions and by the political debate of the 1930's, had been reflected in presidential voting. In 1944 this line of division became blurred as the issues of World War II claimed the attention of voters, only to reassert itself in 1948. The correlation between status and vote declined sharply from

TABLE 4.1. Switches in presidential voting preference, 1948–1952, within groups with specified social and demographic characteristics[a]

Group	% of 1948 D's, D-R		% of 1948 R's, R-D		% of new voters, R	
Economic status						
Average plus	22	(144)	4	(220)	70	(89)
Average	29	(1,363)	5	(1,226)	58	(778)
Poor	21	(1,512)	8	(750)	48	(1,326)
Education						
Grammar school	21	(1,006)	6	(553)	45	(683)
High school	26	(1,163)	6	(797)	52	(858)
College	35	(312)	4	(422)	64	(231)
Race						
White	28	(3,581)	6	(2,575)	54	(2,592)
Colored	13	(276)	19	(72)	23	(270)
Religion						
Protestant	27	(1,486)	4	(1,409)	54	(1,301)
Catholic	24	(804)	9	(337)	45	(401)
Jewish	14	(150)	14	(42)	27	(51)
Occupation						
Business and professional	33	(374)	4	(460)	64	(237)
White-collar	30	(293)	6	(302)	54	(204)
Skilled	26	(421)	11	(136)	54	(320)
Unskilled	19	(1,001)	8	(474)	43	(756)
Farmers and farm laborers	29	(354)	3	(301)	57	(226)

[a] The percentages are based on combinations of 1952 pre-election AIPO surveys. Economic status: 504, 506, and 507. Education: 505, 506, and 507. Race: 504, 505, 506, and 507. Religion: 505, 506, and 507. Occupation: 505, 506, 507. As in earlier chapters, a figure in parentheses is the number of survey respondents on which the percentage is based. To illustrate, the figure 226 at the lower right means that among those interviewed there were 226 farmers and farm laborers who were "new voters" in 1952—that is, for some reason they did not vote in the 1948 presidential election—and 57 per cent of them said they were going to vote for Eisenhower.

1948 to 1952, a step in a trend that was to continue through 1956.[1] In short, in 1952 Republicans picked up strength in the lesser occupational ranks while Democrats gained in the upper occupations, with the result that partisan lines approached less closely occupational or class lines.

By divination from such data on the movements of voters of varying attributes one might conclude that the class tensions of the 1930's had slackened as the New Deal won general acceptance and as the lot of people generally improved. That may have been the case; yet the campaign of 1952 was not without tensions. New concerns replaced old worries, and an unusual degree of political involvement pervaded the electorate. The best index of that involvement may be the expansion of the total presidential vote by about one fourth from 1948 to 1952, an exceptionally high rate of increase which had been last matched in the remarkable growth in turnout from 1924 to 1928.[2] Though explicable in part by a delayed entry into the

1. The pattern from 1944 through 1956 has been analyzed in detail by P. E. Converse, "The Shifting Role of Class in Political Attitudes and Behavior," in *Readings in Social Psychology*, ed. Eleanor Maccoby, Theodore Newcomb, and Eugene Hartley, 3rd ed. (New York: Holt, 1958), pp. 388-399; Angus Campbell *et al.*, *The American Voter* (New York: Wiley, 1960), ch. 13. The decline in association between occupational status and presidential vote is indicated by the following data from surveys by the Survey Research Center of the University of Michigan. They show the Republican percentage of the vote within occupational groups to have been:

	1948	1952	1956
Professional and business	80%	69%	68%
White collar	50	65	62
Skilled and semiskilled	22	44	55
Unskilled	26	31	45

2. The percentage increases in the total presidential vote for elections preceding 1952 were as follows: 1924–28, 25.0; 1928–32, 7.9; 1932–36, 14.9; 1936–40, 9.3; 1940–44, minus 3.9; 1944–48, 1.5; 1948–52, 25.9.

active electorate of potential voters dislocated by World War II, the increase was extraordinary in size and an indication of an above normal intensity of political concern.[3]

It is perilous to make inferences about what voters have or do not have in their minds from observations of the voting behavior of large groups of persons with like attributes: occupation, religion, residence, education. Those inferences are most likely to be correct when the issues and the rhetoric of the campaign happen to affect directly and clearly persons of particular kinds. When those conditions are fulfilled, gross characteristics of individuals, which are easily obtained in survey interviews, may serve handily as an indication of attitudes. Yet the fact that a person is, say, a Negro serves as an index to what he believes and to why he votes as he does only when an election concerns Negroes as Negroes and when the members of the group are aware of the issue and see it as basic among their concerns of the moment. Not every election generates group-related issues which drive a wedge through the electorate along lines easily identified by gross characteristics of the electorate. About what the data of Table 4.1 suggest is that the 1952 election divided people differently than did the preceding elections and that if one wishes to understand the election he should examine directly attitudes about issues and other questions of the campaign rather than attempt to deduce motivation from gross characteristics of voters.[4]

3. The 1952 AIPO post-election survey showed 20 per cent of the voters to be 1948 nonvoters. This is surely an underestimate. The known increase of 25 per cent in the vote from 1948 to 1952 would have produced a voting population with 20 per cent of its members 1948 nonvoters even with no allowance for mortality between 1948 and 1952 or for nonvoting in 1952 by 1948 voters.
4. One inference from the data of Table 4.1 does seem plausible. Note that Negro Democrats of 1948 defected in 1952 at a lower rate

When one examines directly the policy preferences of voters and the relation of those preferences to the vote, some of the puzzling features of the election of 1952—and of the American party system generally—begin to make themselves evident. Eisenhower's victory seems to have been at bottom a victory that rested on a transient majority which could exist no longer than the issues around which it was built. On the great and continuing economic questions of domestic policy a popular majority remained hostile to the Republican position—as it saw that position. Once circumstances developed to restore those issues to the forefront, the Eisenhower majority would be in danger unless it had managed in the meanwhile to alter the majority impression of its position on those questions.

With the advantages of hindsight such an interpretation can be read into the electoral attitudes toward labor-management rivalry in 1952. In the closing years of the Truman Administration friction between employers and workers increased in scope and intensity. That increase was one of fact and not simply one of political rhetoric. The average annual number of "work stoppages" in 1950–1952 exceeded by 37 per cent the annual average in 1947–1949.[5] In the confrontation of employer and employee, the

---

than any other group listed, whereas 1948 Republican Negroes had the highest R-D rate in the table. President Truman had stoutly and conspicuously stood for civil rights, a question doubtless salient in the thoughts of many Negro voters. Moreover, events of the 1952 Democratic convention made the party's commitment plain. To conclude that these stimuli played upon the members of the group and produced the observed effects, one must assume that the members of the group had a sense of group identification and an awareness of group-relevant stimuli, conditions by no means invariably met but which may have prevailed for Negroes in 1952. See the discussion by Angus Campbell *et al.*, *The American Voter*, ch. 12.

5. The figures from the Bureau of Labor Statistics on the numbers of work stoppages were: 1947, 3,693; 1948, 3,419; 1949, 3,606; 1950, 4,843; 1951, 4,737; 1952, 5,117; 1953, 5,091; 1954, 3,468.

Administration was doubtless seen as on the side of the worker—and also as accountable for its failure to keep industrial peace. That perception received powerful reinforcement in the 1952 seizure by the President of strike-threatened steel mills whose output was required for military purposes. His action, taken in the absence of explicit statutory authority, found disfavor with the Supreme Court—as well as with a goodly sector of the population.

How did the voters react to the turmoil in industrial relations? During the campaign Dr. Gallup's interviewers put the following question: "In the labor disputes of the last two or three years, have your sympathies, in general, been on the side of the unions or on the side of the companies?" Most 1948 Truman voters, as would have been expected, sympathized with the unions, and most 1948 Dewey voters inclined in their sentiments to favor the companies. Of those 1948 Democrats who sympathized with the companies, though, almost half announced an intention to vote Republican in 1952, a defection rate about three times as great as that among union sympathizers. On the other hand, though few 1948 Republicans defected in 1952, those sympathetic toward unions were about four times as likely to vote for Stevenson as were company sympathizers. The data appear in Table 4.2.[6]

Though Eisenhower picked up votes on the labor issue at the election of 1952, the general balance of sympathies between the unions and the companies also pointed to a weakness of the Eisenhower electoral support. Despite the fact that a substantial majority of those sympathetic to the companies supported Eisenhower, a substantial

6. Similar findings came from the question: "Do you think the Taft-Hartley law should be left as it is, changed, or done away with?" Of those 1948 Truman voters who thought it should be "left as is," about half expressed a 1952 preference for Eisenhower. AIPO 505-TPS, 10-3-52. The Democratic platform advocated the repeal of the Taft-Hartley Act.

TABLE 4.2. Switches in presidential voting preference, 1948–1952, in relation to response to question: "In the labor disputes of the last two or three years, have your sympathies, in general, been on the side of the unions or on the side of the companies?"[a]

Response	% of 1948 D's, D-R	% of 1948 R's, R-D	% of new voters, R
Companies	47 (440)	4 (768)	72 (426)
Unions	16 (1,251)	16 (353)	39 (636)
Both	32 (65)	11 (61)	[b]
No opinion	30 (515)	6 (401)	52 (344)

[a] A consolidation of AIPO 506, 10-7-52, and 507K, 10-15-52.
[b] Less than 50 cases.

majority of the entire electorate sympathized with the unions (as examination of the parenthesized N's in Table 4.2 will indicate). The inference is plausible that a majority of the voters regarded other matters as more important at the moment than industrial relations. And a plausible expectation would have been that when circumstances came about to make that complex of issues involved in the capital-labor relation salient, a good deal of Republican support would disappear, given the picture of the Republican party implanted in the public mind. The popular partisan majority was not congruent with the latent popular majority on the basic issue of the relations of capital and labor.[7]

7. On the basis of data on a wider range of issues, Angus Campbell has pointed out that the 1952 D-R switchers differed in their policy outlooks from the Republican regulars. They also retained a sense of identification with the Democratic party. See Angus Campbell, Gerald Gurin, and W. E. Miller, *The Voter Decides* (Evanston, Ill.: Row, Peterson, 1954), ch. 12. One does not build a theory on a single case, but a theory of systemic dissonance may fit one aspect of the behavior of the American party system. The greater the departures from congruity between policy majorities and electoral majorities, the less secure is the electoral majority. A degree of incongruity is inevitable in a two-party system, but exceptional circumstances which reduce attitudes on broad and basic issues to temporary latency may produce electoral majorities of exceptional fragility.

Dissatisfaction with the conduct of foreign affairs damaged the Democratic cause in 1952. Anxieties about the Korean war and about "Communism" both domestic and global reinforced each other to produce defections from the Democratic ranks. Those 1948 Republicans who saw our entry into the Korean war as a mistake were strengthened in their adherence to the Republican party. And, in a pattern that recurs in our tables, those 1948 Republicans who concurred with Democratic actions rarely were sufficiently moved thereby to desert their customary voting position. The most notable impact of the Korean issue appeared among the many 1948 Democrats who regarded our entry into the Korean war as a mistake. About four out of ten of such persons preferred Eisenhower in 1952, a rate of defection about twice as great as among those who thought we had not erred in getting into the war.[8] The details appear in Table 4.3.

Though determining the relation between views on these specific policy questions and the vote gives us clues to the motivation of voters, perhaps all the issues the voter faced in 1952 were bundled up in the question whether he approved of the performance of the party in power. And that became in reality a question of whether he approved of Mr. Truman. Not surprisingly, few 1948 Republicans viewed favorably the way Mr. Truman was handling his job as president; most of them were reinforced in their Republicanism by their estimate of Democratic performance. The rub came in the attitudes of 1948 nonvoters and 1948 Democrats. Over a third of the

8. Apparently the campaign converted the Korean affair into a major issue. In an open-ended question the percentages mentioning the Korean issue as one of the most important problems facing the country were: June, 30; September, 33; mid-October, 39; late October, 52. Louis Harris, *Is There a Republican Majority?* (New York: Harper, 1954), p. 25.

TABLE 4.3. Switches in presidential voting preference, 1948–1952, in relation to response to question: "Do you think the U.S. made a mistake in going into the war in Korea or not?"[a]

Response	% of 1948 D's, D-R		% of 1948 R's, R-D		% of new voters, R	
Yes, mistake	37	(821)	5	(912)	64	(622)
No	20	(1,032)	11	(462)	46	(550)
No opinion	18	(420)	9	(205)	38	(247)

[a] Based on a consolidation of AIPO 506K, 10-7-52, and 507K, 10-15-52.

1948 Democrats in 1952 disapproved of Truman's performance and about half of this group said they would vote for Eisenhower. Of those who had not voted in 1948, over half looked with disfavor upon Mr. Truman and about three fourths of these dour individuals preferred Eisenhower. And, it will be remembered, the number of new voters in 1952 was exceptionally large. The details are shown in Table 4.4.[9]

The election of 1952 may thus be more than plausibly characterized as a verdict of dissatisfaction with the past performance of the Democratic Administration. It may, of course, be said that a vote against Mr. Stevenson because one disapproved of Mr. Truman's performance represented an irrational act. Mr. Truman, after all, was not the candidate. Moreover, Mr. Stevenson went to some pains to attempt to disassociate himself from the Truman Administration. He maintained a separate campaign headquarters in Springfield and in other ways sought to estab-

9. The importance of the public impression of Democratic performance is confirmed by the findings of Angus Campbell and his associates. They identified, by the analysis of responses to open-ended questions, a dimension of attitude which they called attitude "toward parties as managers of government." By what was essentially a content analysis of responses in interviews, popular attitudes on this dimension were shown to be strongly anti-Democratic and pro-Republican. See Campbell et al., The American Voter, ch. 19.

TABLE 4.4. Switches in presidential voting preference, 1948–1952, in relation to response to question: "Do you approve or disapprove of the way Truman is handling his job as President?"[a]

Response	% of 1948 D's, D-R		% of 1948 R's, R-D		% of new voters, R	
Approve	10	(1,290)	35	(97)	23	(712)
Disapprove	55	(985)	4	(1,673)	73	(1,092)
No opinion	26	(285)	12	(90)	40	(237)

[a] A consolidation of AIPO 504, 10-1-52; 505-TPS, 10-3-52; 506, 10-7-52.

lish himself in the public mind as independent of the Truman Administration. Yet voters—or a significant number of them—voted against Mr. Stevenson because they disapproved of Mr. Truman, despite Mr. Stevenson's most adroit efforts in evasion and avoidance. It is well that a political party cannot avoid accountability for its past performance. The only really effective weapon of popular control in a democratic regime is the capacity of the electorate to throw a party from power. Not only was Mr. Stevenson rejected; other Democrats also fell by the wayside and the party leadership collectively lost, at least for a time, the fruits of power. In effect, many Democrats felt the effects of public dissatisfaction with their party's performance. Had Mr. Stevenson not been saddled with responsibility for past Democratic performance—or were other like-situated candidates not usually so saddled—the electorate would be deprived of its most effective instrument for control of governments. Happily, too, this institutional custom probably permits the electorate to be utilized to best advantage in the process of popular government. The odds are that the electorate as a whole is better able to make a retrospective appraisal of the work of governments than it is to make estimates of the future performance of nonincumbent candidates. Yet by virtue of the combination of the electorate's retrospective judgment and the custom of party accountability, the electorate can exert a prospective influence if not control. Governments must worry, not about the meaning of past elections, but about their fate at future elections.

The election of 1952 may illustrate the role of the electorate as judge and executioner. It, too, suggests observations about the requisites the minority party must fulfill if it is to play its role in a two-party system. We must have, the commonplace axiom goes, an active minority party so that when necessity arises an outraged citizenry can use it as an instrument to replace the majority and, incidentally, to punish it by banishment. But not just any sort of minority will serve the purpose. If it is to be serviceable, the minority must not clearly threaten basic policies that have won majority acceptance. The Republican party met these conditions in 1952, not so much through its own internal reform as through the special qualities of its candidate. And the odds are that Eisenhower won, not so much because of his "personality" as because certain of his qualities happened to dovetail nicely with the requirements of the situation in which the country and the Republican party found itself. Simple interpretations of Republican defeats in the elections of 1940, 1944, and 1948 are suspect, but undoubtedly a factor of considerable importance was the failure of Republican campaigners to persuade enough people that the G.O.P. regarded the major elements of the New Deal as matters of settled public policy. Dewey in 1944 and 1948 became the first genuine "me too" candidate, but the country did not regard him as believable in that role, perhaps in 1948 in major part because of the performance of the Republican Congress elected in 1946. Nor had the Republican party succeeded in erasing from the public mind its image as irresponsibly isolationist.

In 1952 the Republican party converted itself into a

minority that could be used by a majority disposed to make a change. Eisenhower's views on domestic policy were hazy, but his dramatic victory over Senator Taft for the nomination made it plausible for people to suppose that his views differed from those of Taft who had come to symbolize orthodox Republicanism. The same event along with Eisenhower's experience in NATO and his views on foreign policy made it difficult for him to be attacked as isolationist. In short, Eisenhower's nomination put a new face on the party. In addition, his military and diplomatic experience made him appear to be the better man to cope with the immediate diplomatic and military problems that the country faced. And this quality aided in drawing erstwhile Democratic voters to his support, as the data of Table 4.5 suggest.

The entire episode throws light on the qualities that a minority must possess if it is to serve its purpose. A minority led by radical conservatives probably would have had great difficulty in winning in 1952. This is not to say that a serviceable minority must be identical with the majority; it must be different. It must be different enough in the appropriate aspect to arouse hope that it can cope satisfactorily with those problems on which the majority has

TABLE 4.5. Switches in presidential voting preference, 1948–1952, in relation to response to question: "Which presidential candidate—Stevenson or Eisenhower—do you think could handle the Korean situation best?"[a]

Response	% of 1948 D's, D-R	% of 1948 R's, R-D	% of new voters, R
Stevenson	1 (364)	92 (12)	2 (165)
Eisenhower	50 (546)	3 (739)	76 (513)
No difference	6 (101)	36 (22)	18 (68)
No opinion	12 (96)	29 (21)	23 (52)

[a] AIPO 506, 10-7-52. Obviously, no weight should be given to the percentages for the cells with quite small N's.

flunked. It must not, though, so threaten accepted policies and practices that it arouses widespread anxieties. The circumstances of 1952 made the Republican party for the nonce a usable minority—in a country normally Democratic.

The campaign of 1956, a rerun of the 1952 race between Eisenhower and Stevenson, occurred under circumstances generally favorable to the Republican party. Eisenhower had gone to Korea and had made a settlement of sorts that won public acclaim, though it was of a kind that envious Democrats asserted the country would not have accepted at their hands. Furthermore, since 1952 average family income had been on an upward trend; such expressions of economic discontent as were heard came from farmers. The congressional election of 1954 had checked the moves of the more conservative wing of the Republican party for a sharp turn to the right in domestic policy. Democratic campaigners could not build up Eisenhower into a threat to the social gains achieved under Democratic auspices; Eisenhower had become a benign and beloved figure who was in a sense above politics. Indeed, in the situation in which he found himself by 1956 he was the chieftain of a crusade that he could lead neither to the left nor to the right, even if he had been so disposed.

On the foreign front, too, the march of events, though disquieting, could not be converted into a telling indictment of the Republican Administration. The Senate reprimand of Senator Joseph McCarthy in 1954 had led to a reduction in the ear-splitting clamor about the management of foreign affairs. The death of Stalin in 1953 and the move toward the destruction of the Stalin myth in the 1956 Soviet Party Congress generated some hope that the tone, if not the substance, of Soviet foreign policy might change. In June 1956, Polish workers rose in revolt in

Poznan; the Administration's hands-off policy removed any fear that the 1952 campaign hints of aid to the satellites might involve us in a war. Other occurrences in the days immediately preceding the election reinforced the affirmations of Republican campaigners that the moment was inappropriate for a change in the control of foreign policy. In July, Premier Nasser of Egypt had seized the Suez Canal. Discussions ensued which eventually exhausted the patience of the French and British who grasped control of the canal on the eve of the American election. At the same time Israeli forces moved into the Sinai Peninsula and wiped out Egyptian resistance. Shortly before, in October, the Hungarian uprising had been crushed by Soviet military forces. Thus, in the weeks and days immediately before the polling, outbreaks scattered over the globe indicated the existence of a volatile situation that might get out of hand without firm handling; and no Administration action in the foreign field could be made to appear to be an obvious and major blunder. Under these circumstances, Democrats might speak with horror of John Foster Dulles' practice of "brinksmanship," but they could really make no effective major attack on the Republican record.

The voters continued Eisenhower in office by an increased plurality; he polled 57.8 per cent of the two-party vote against 55.4 per cent in 1952. The vote expressed, if not overwhelming confidence in Eisenhower's performance, certainly a preference for him over Stevenson under the circumstances of the time. What popular attitude toward the Republican party the election reflected is another matter. Blessed with an exceptionally popular incumbent president, Republicans failed to win a majority of the House seats, perhaps an indication of both the weakness of the party and of the personal strength of the President.

The seemingly negligible net movement of 2.4 per cent in the vote from 1952 to 1956 resulted from a far larger amount of switching to and fro across party lines than the figure itself suggests. To a considerable extent these movements grew from the impact of specific policies and actions upon voter preferences. Rates of switching reported by various categories of voters appear in Table 4.6. The broad pattern is roughly the obverse of that which prevailed when Democratic candidates sought a continuation of power. In those elections, as the tables of Chapter 3 indicated, the support of the party in power ebbed

TABLE 4.6. Switches in presidential voting preference, 1952–1956, within groups with specified social and demographic characteristics[a]

Group	% of 1952 R's, R-D		% of 1952 D's, D-R		% of new voters, R	
Occupation						
Business and professional	14	(281)	11	(104)	52	(87)
White-collar	18	(151)	8	(88)	47	(81)
Skilled	15	(157)	7	(109)	42	(87)
Unskilled	17	(237)	7	(214)	46	(200)
Farmers and farm laborers	32	(116)	5	(58)	45	(53)
Education						
Grammar school	19	(762)	7	(468)	51	(541)
High school	13	(1,325)	8	(761)	50	(770)
College	11	(573)	10	(196)	59	(179)
Race						
White	16	(1,821)	9	(903)	50	(953)
Colored	25	(72)	12	(90)	47	(144)
Religion						
Protestant	14	(2,029)	10	(689)	53	(850)
Catholic	21	(624)	9	(464)	44	(265)
Jewish	33	(46)	4	(76)	20	(15)

[a] Based on consolidations of AIPO polls. Occupation and race: 572 and 573. Education and religion: 571, 572, and 573.

away and replacements had to be sought from opposition supporters and from new voters. In 1956 the Republican party, as the party in power, began to experience an attrition from among its supporters of four years before. It had to convert 1952 Stevenson voters and win new voters to its cause. In that endeavor, on balance, it increased, over 1952, its proportion of the two-party vote, though its success probably was greater among "old" voters than "new" voters.[10]

Moreover, the pattern of Republican defections in relation to status was the reverse of that which had earlier affected Democratic support. Defections from the Democratic following, it will be remembered, declined from group to group as one went down the status ladder, in accord with the supposition that Democratic policies might most effectively reinforce the partisan loyalties of lower-status voters. From 1952 to 1956, however, the Republican defection pattern tended, less clearly and sharply, to increase step by step down the status scale, a pattern that appears most markedly in the education data in Table 4.6.[11] Defections from Eisenhower occurred at the highest rate among persons with a grammar school

10. The data underlying Table 4.6 show that Eisenhower attracted in 1956 a larger proportion of the 1952 voters than of "new" voters. Roper poll 65, October 1956, showed a similar though not so wide difference. These are, of course, pre-election data and the differential may not have prevailed in the actual voting.

11. A glance at Table 4.6 may leave one skeptical that such a pattern of switching could occur and still leave enough of a Republican vote for Eisenhower to win. A check, though, of the figures underlying the analysis by race (which most nearly encompasses the entire sample) shows that the switchers, standpatters, and new voters balance out to 55.9 per cent for Eisenhower, only slightly under the actual election percentage. That discrepancy could be regarded as further support for the hunch that all our data overestimate the actual degree of switching, as support for the belief that in 1956 Eisenhower picked up some strength in the last days of the campaign, or as evidence of imprecision of measurement.

education and at the lowest among his 1952 supporters with college training, differentials that might be expected of a competition between orthodox Democratic and Republican doctrines.[12] Whatever the reason, the fact that the different circumstances of 1956 produced a pattern of switching unlike that of 1940 gives us some confidence in our data. It suggests that deliberate choices, appropriate to differing circumstances, underlie the movements of voters that our tables record rather than a special disposition by members of particular sectors of the population to report a switch to poll interviewers.[13]

12. The same pattern of defection appears in the Roper poll's categorization of respondents according to economic level. The percentages of R-D defectors, 1952–56, for the specified economic levels were: B, 8; C, 12; D, 19. On the other hand, the D-R defection percentages were: B, 19; C, 11; D, 8. The N's for the A level were too small to produce trustworthy percentages. Roper poll 65, October 1956.

13. It is probably a sound guess that there is a category of persons without much political information or involvement that in almost a frictionless manner moves with shifts in the predominant stimuli of their environment; that group, though, is not defined by demographic attributes. Something of a case can be made, however, for the proposition that voting volatility declines with age. Within the specified age groups, the percentages switching, either D-R or R-D, as reported in pre-election polls for the indicated elections were as follows:

	21–39	40–59	60 and over
1940	20	17	14
1944	15	16	13
1948	22	18	14
1952	21	17	14
1956	15	14	11
1960	23	24	16

Whether age really produces these small differences in switching rates is another question. The relative stability of voting preference in the older age groups may reflect both the stability of the alternatives posed by elections over this period and the stability of status and interest acquired by the individual as he ages. The test of the bearing of age as such on voting would occur in an election that raised novel and salient issues pulling against the customary voting habits of older persons. That is, given good reason to switch, the older age groups might not turn out to be any more stable than younger voters. See the related discussion by Angus Campbell *et al., The American Voter*, pp. 161-165.

Under the conditions of world politics of the months preceding the 1956 election, foreign politics might plausibly have been expected to be foremost in the mind of the electorate. The record of the Eisenhower Administration—and perhaps the hesitation to change horses in the middle of a tense moment—gave the Republican candidate a marked edge on this question. Dr. Gallup's interviewers asked during the campaign: "Which political party do you think would be more likely to keep the United States out of World War III—the Republican party or the Democratic party?" Among those with opinions, the Republican party won the nod by a substantial margin, though the evidence of other surveys suggests that by the Republican party the respondents really meant President Eisenhower and not the party. A few 1952 Republicans had arrived at the conclusion that Mr. Stevenson could handle the situation better than President Eisenhower and a large proportion of these few expressed a preference for Adlai. And a few 1952 Democrats came to believe that Eisenhower could better cope with foreign affairs and a substantial proportion of them reported a switch to Eisenhower. Judgment on the relative competence of the parties in foreign affairs seemed to be especially influential on the vote of "new" voters, as the details of Table 4.7 indicate.

The available data do not permit the pursuit of the question of the impact on the electorate of specific aspects of foreign affairs, but one survey, conducted before the British and French response to the seizure of the Suez Canal, gives a clue to the voter reaction to one aspect of foreign policy. A large majority of those who had "heard of the Suez Canal problem" and had opinions about it approved "of the way Secretary Dulles is handling the

84

TABLE 4.7. Switches in presidential voting preference, 1952–1956, in relation to response to question: "Which political party do you think would be more likely to keep the United States out of World War III—the Republican party or the Democratic party?"[a]

Response	% of 1952 R's, R-D		% of 1952 D's, D-R		% of new voters, R	
Republican	4	(1,279)	39	(122)	85	(432)
Democratic	79	(108)	2	(426)	10	(239)
Same	37	(253)	6	(263)	35	(147)
No opinion	42	(141)	5	(166)	44	(172)

[a] A consolidation of AIPO 571K, 9-18-56, and 573K, 10-16-56.

problem." Of those 1952 Republicans who disapproved, though, about half announced that they would vote for Stevenson, and a less marked countermovement occurred among 1952 Democratic voters who looked with approbation on the Secretary's performance.[14] While Democratic approvers were more likely than Democratic disapprovers to defect to Eisenhower, most approvers remained Democratic, as Table 4.8 shows. That pattern—among the outs —of approval yet retention of an opposition voting posture occurs in our data on many, perhaps most, issues and may point to a basic factor of ameliorative significance in American politics. An Administration may expect to win the policy support of many opposition followers even though it cannot win their vote at the next election. That fact contributes to the blurring of the distinctions between

14. If one regarded the measure as precise and attributed all the loss associated with disapproval of Dulles' handling of Suez to that fact, the loss was by no means negligible politically. The total N for AIPO 571, on which Table 4.8 is based, was 2,208. The 37 respondents (45 per cent of 82) reporting a 1952 Republican vote, dissatisfaction with Suez, and a switch to Stevenson amounted to 1.7 per cent of the total sample.

TABLE 4.8. Switching in presidential voting preference, 1952–1956, among those who had heard of the Suez Canal problem, in relation to response to question: "Do you approve of the way Secretary Dulles is handling the problem?"[a]

Response	% of 1952 R's, R-D	% of 1952 D's, D-R	% of new voters, R
Approve	11 (465)	13 (124)	69 (172)
Disapprove	45 (82)	2 (127)	36 (47)
No opinion	17 (271)	8 (177)	53 (173)

[a] AIPO 571, 9-18-56.

parties and, probably thereby, to the mitigation of the sharpness of partisan conflict in the eras between elections.[15]

The generally healthy state of the economy in 1956 doubtless made the issue of prosperity something less than the primary focus of voter interest. On the question of which party would "do the best job of keeping the country prosperous" over the next few years, Republicans and Democrats stood about neck and neck in the population generally, in contrast with the marked Republican advantage on the prospects for keeping the peace. Eisenhower had calmed the anxieties of many persons who had believed that Republican rule and depressions inevitably went together. Nevertheless, doubts remained which would be intensified when appropriate circumstances arose. In the movements across party lines from 1952 to

15. The electoral response to the Suez affair probably turns up also in the data of Table 4.6. Note that, though the N's are small, the highest R-D defection rate for 1952–56 in the table occurred among 1952 Jewish Republican voters, while the lowest D-R defection rate occurred among 1952 Jewish Democratic voters. The Eisenhower Administration in its handling of the Egyptian affair and other related episodes in the Middle East aroused no great acclaim in the American Jewish community.

1956, though, a high association prevailed with appraisals of prospective party performance. Those few 1952 Democrats who thought the Republican party could do a better job of keeping the country prosperous switched in high degree as did those of the more numerous body of 1952 Republican voters whose experience with Eisenhower led them to the opposite conclusion. The precise movements are set out in Table 4.9.

The most conspicuous holdout from the surge of public approbation that met President Eisenhower as he sought re-election was the farmer. Over broad areas of the farming country of the Middle West, Eisenhower polled a smaller proportion of the vote than he had in 1952. In the nation as a whole, as Table 4.6 showed, Eisenhower suffered a greater attrition of 1952 support among farmers than in any other major occupational category. A sharp and prolonged decline in farm prices had gotten under way about the time the Republicans took power. In part, changes in the supply-demand situation brought about this decline. In part, though, Republican revisions of agri-

TABLE 4.9. Switches in presidential voting preference, 1952–1956, in relation to response to question: "Looking ahead for the next few years, which political party—the Republican or the Democratic—do you think will do the best job of keeping the country prosperous?"[a]

Response	% of 1952 D's, D-R	% of 1952 R's, R-D	% of new voters, R
Republican	73 (56)	1 (1,191)	96 (349)
Democratic	3 (793)	76 (278)	12 (443)
Same	10 (78)	20 (181)	55 (92)
No opinion	18 (74)	22 (179)	70 (70)

[a] A consolidation of AIPO 571K, 9-18-56, and 573K, 10-16-56.

cultural policy accounted for the price drop, especially in the case of those commodities for which government price supports were reduced. Farmer anxieties also fed on fears of the future as the Republican leadership advocated a course of action which would lead to subjection of the farmer to the cold and forbidding winds of the free market. Ezra Taft Benson, the Secretary of Agriculture, personified the new Republican agricultural policy. He fought with dedication, but not with notable success, to advance his views and to defend the Administration policy against Democratic critics. Republican Senators and Representatives, especially those from farming states, soon came to regard Secretary Benson as a political liability, but he doggedly stuck to his guns with the steadfast support of the President. Probably around one third of 1952 Republican farm voters turned Democratic in their 1956 preference, while only a few 1952 Democratic farm voters could find reason to support Eisenhower in 1956. The erosion of Republican farm support seemed to have been closely associated with attitudes toward Secretary Benson. In September 1956, *Wallace's Farmer* asked its sample of Iowa farmers: "On the basis of his record, what kind of a job as Secretary of Agriculture would you expect Ezra T. Benson to do if he continues in office another four years?" The probability that 1952 Republican farm voters would stay with Eisenhower varied with their appraisal of the prospective performance of Mr. Benson. About half of those who could see him doing only a poor job intended to switch to the Democrats; those with a high regard for Mr. Benson remained loyal Republicans in high degree, as Table 4.10 indicates. Leaders of the American Farm Bureau Federation stood firmly by Secretary Benson, whose goals generally paralleled those of the Federation;

TABLE 4.10. Iowa farmers and Ezra Taft Benson: Switches in presidential voting preference, 1952–1956, in relation to response to question: "On the basis of his record, what kind of a job as Secretary of Agriculture would you expect Ezra T. Benson to do if he continues in office another four years?"[a]

Response	% of 1952 R's, R-D	% of 1952 D's, D-R
Good	5 (62)	0 (5)
Fair	27 (52)	0 (16)
Poor	50 (64)	2 (88)
Not sure	18 (33)	[b] (10)

[a] *Wallace's Farmer*, survey #6, September 1956.
[b] One respondent in this cell reported a shift to Eisenhower.

it is doubtful that their endeavors materially helped the Republican cause.[16]

In 1956 talk of the cult of personality came from many journalistic commentators, as well as from Democrats. These learned observers psychoanalyzed the population and concluded that American politics could be explained as a manifestation of the power of the father image. One may doubt the necessity of resorting to such dubious hypotheses to explain the response of the electorate to the situation; yet undoubtedly popular evaluations of President Eisenhower played an important role in the voting in 1956. Using data and methods different from those employed here, Angus Campbell and his associates have shown that popular attitudes of approbation toward Eisenhower bulked large in the public mind in 1956, even more predominantly than the popular perception of the Republican party's superiority in foreign affairs. The Demo-

16. A consolidation of *Wallace's Farmer* polls of September and October 1956 showed the following percentages of 1952 Republican farm voters switching to a Democratic preference: Farm Bureau members, 27; nonmembers, 34.

cratic party remained, though, in 1956 as it had been in 1952, the party which was most commonly seen as more likely to look out for group interests, i.e., the "common man," workers, Negroes, or "ordinary people like me."[17] Once these group concerns became salient in the voters' minds, the predominance of pro-Democratic popular attitudes with respect to them would weaken the Republican combination.[18]

All in all, the polling of 1956 must be interpreted as a vote of confidence for Eisenhower and the presidential wing of the Republican party, if not for the Republican party generally. His gain in popular plurality concealed a more complex pattern of gains and losses. Accountability for the exercise of power produced its inevitable attrition as those dissatisfied with particular actions defected to the Democratic cause, a movement perhaps of most electoral significance among farmers. The exercise of power also had its effects in reinforcing the loyalties of most 1952 Republican voters as well as in recruiting a few 1952 Democratic voters. Confidence in Eisenhower as a person better able to cope with the problems of the time pervaded the process of electoral decision and doubtless contributed to the result.

Our information about the 1952 behavior of voters throws some light on a problem that bemuses theorists of

17. *The American Voter,* ch. 19. For a more extensive account of the findings on these points, see D. E. Stokes, Angus Campbell, and W. E. Miller, "Components of Electoral Decision," *American Political Science Review,* 52 (1958), 367-387.

18. Eisenhower's health concerned some voters in 1956. His heart attack of 1955 and his ileitis operation of 1956 made some voters doubt that his health would permit him to carry on the responsibility of the presidency for another four years. In early October about half of those 1952 Republican voters with these doubts preferred Stevenson. AIPO 572, 10-5-56.

democratic institutions. That is the problem of what kinds of people make workable a system of competitive party politics. One could imagine majority and minority groupings so doctrinaire and so fixed in their partisan loyalties that the political system would have no flexibility. "Normal" democratic processes would languish, so cohesive would be the following of the majority party; the majority would win every election. As the system now exists, of course, many voters have strong party loyalties. They vote Democratic—or Republican—whatever the circumstances, though perhaps not so foolishly as is often supposed, for this strong partisan attachment seems to be associated in high degree with compatible policy outlooks and expectations. Nevertheless, many voters do switch from party to party and in sufficient numbers from time to time to replace one party by another in control of the government. Obviously the switchers play a significant role in a democratic system, for they permit, if they do not bring about, those major adjustments that occur in the system. Moreover, they contribute fundamentally to the process by which the people in a democratic order can discipline and keep somewhat responsive to popular wishes those who happen to occupy positions of authority. Speculators about the nature of democratic processes ask who the switchers are, what their motivations are, what their social characteristics are, what peculiar social environmental influences move them, and so forth.

These and related questions commentators answer with more assurance than data. At one time the publicists asserted that upper-class independents, well informed and dedicated to the general weal, deliberated on the issues of the day in a disinterested way and decided the fate of candidates. This explanation fell before the criticism of the analysts of electoral behavior whose researches identified the characteristics of the "independent" voter. Their independent voter, however, was a product of their definition. "Independent" came to be defined as one of several categories of voters arrayed along a scale of party identification. Some persons proclaim themselves to be strong Democrats or strong Republicans. Others appraise themselves as not such strong partisans and thereby permit themselves to be categorized as weak Democrats or weak Republicans. Of those who claim that they are independents, some will concede that they lean Democratic or Republican. A few remain—5 to 10 per cent of the electorate —who stubbornly insist that they are independents with no leanings in either partisan direction. This group of genuine "independents" is not an impressive lot. On the average, its level of information is low, its sense of political involvement is slight, its level of political participation is not high, its decision on how to vote is made late in the campaign, and its sense of political efficacy is quite low. Moreover, these "independents" manifest a striking electoral volatility and, insofar as they vote, tend to move in high degree toward the prevailing side.[19]

Some observers move bravely to the conclusion that the fate of the Republic rests in the hands of an ignorant and uninformed sector of the electorate highly susceptible to influence by factors irrelevant to the solemn performance of its civic duties. That conclusion is certainly not invariably, if ever, correct. In the election of 1952, an election with an unusually marked amount of party switching, this repulsive type of "independent" did not call the turn. Among the switchers from Truman to Eisenhower he was far outnumbered by people who regarded themselves as

19. On some of the characteristics of the independent, see Campbell *et al., The American Voter*, pp. 143-145.

Democrats, as Angus Campbell has shown.[20] Yet we are left with the fact that many voters, whether they call themselves Democrats, Republicans, or independents, cross party lines from election to election. Enough of them are inconstant in their partisan attachments to shift the balance of power from time to time.

These party switchers—be they independents in the sense mentioned above, or Republicans, or Democrats—contribute useful properties to the political system rather than endanger the Republic, at least in the judgment of some careful students. Bernard Berelson points out that the highly interested voters "vote more, and know more about the campaign, and participate more."[21] They are, though, less likely to change and less open to persuasion, dispositions which, extended far enough, could produce a fatal rigidity in the political system. The "least admirable" voters contribute a necessary flexibility to the system. Those who "most readily" change voting preferences "are those who are least interested, who are subject to conflicting social pressures, who have inconsistent beliefs and erratic voting histories."[22] And the apathetic have "probably helped to hold the system together and cushioned the shock of disagreement, adjustment, and change."[23]

These propositions require modification in the light of the data analyzed in these chapters. The necessary modifications put a different light on the characteristics of the

20. Campbell *et al., The Voter Decides,* ch. 12.
21. Bernard R. Berelson, Paul F. Lazarsfeld, and William N. McPhee, *Voting* (Chicago: University of Chicago Press, 1954), p. 314.
22. *Ibid.,* p. 316.
23. *Ibid.,* p. 322. Talcott Parsons has constructed a model of the political system incorporating the notion of the role of the shifting indifferent in elections. See his " 'Voting' and the Equilibrium of the American Political System," in E. J. Burdick and A. J. Brodbeck, *American Voting Behavior* (Glencoe, Ill.: Free Press, 1959), pp. 80-120.

switching voters, those who introduce a degree of flexibility in the political system as a whole. The apparent conflicts between our extensive body of data and that on which Berelson based his tentative theoretical propositions can probably be reconciled.[24] The theoretical propositions extrapolated from the data by Berelson, and more especially the theoretical notions propounded by some less cautious students who have built on his findings, need to be carefully reconsidered. That reconsideration must, it now seems, lead to the conclusion that the sector of the electorate which introduces flexibility and play into the political system diverges in its characteristics rather markedly in at least some respects from the "least admirable" voters described by Berelson.

Level of education serves as a handy index of population characteristics and we can readily contrast the educational levels of our various categories of voters. In their average level of education switchers do not differ significantly from standpatters. At least they did not in the election of 1952. Switchers from Republican to Democratic included a slightly higher proportion of persons with college education than did the 1948–1952 Democratic standpatters. Switchers from Democratic to Republican included slightly fewer college-trained persons than did the 1948–1952 Republican standpat group. Each group of

24. The reconciliation of the apparent conflicts in the data are hypothetical but perhaps correct. Berelson concerns himself with "change" in voting intention over the period of a campaign (as determined by a sequence of interviews of the same persons); the data we are examining concern change over a four-year period. Those persons who switch before the campaign begins may differ from those whose voting intention shifts during the campaign. Our data, too, suffer from the uncertainties induced by doubts about the validity of the recall of the vote of four years before. Berelson's findings rest on the data of the campaign of 1948, and switching voters (however defined) may differ in their characteristics among campaigns with their contrasting impacts upon the electorate.

switchers thus retained some of the characteristics of the group from which it had defected. Nor did the "new" voters differ materially from the standpatters of the party for which they expressed a preference, though the "new" voters with a Republican preference included a slightly smaller proportion of persons with college training than did the standpat Republican group. These comparisons appear in detail in Table 4.11.

Another way to use the data on education is to ask the question whether highly educated persons are more likely to switch, in one direction or the other, than persons with less formal education. The proportions of persons of the specified educational levels reporting a switch in presidential preference (either R-D or D-R) in pre-election surveys before several elections follow:

	College	High school	Grade school
1940–44[25]	11%	11%	9%
1948–52	17	18	16
1952–56	11	13	14
1956–60	17	21	22

From these figures one can scarcely argue that party-switching rates vary notably, either positively or negatively, with level of education. About all that the slight differences suggest is that party switching is associated with factors other than how long a person attended school and that those factors must differ from election to election. Perhaps the major such factor, as our many tables in this and the preceding chapter make abundantly clear, is that of the issues and kindred questions. If the issues fall in

25. The 1940–44 figures are based on NORC 30/229, October 1944. The others rest on consolidations of AIPO surveys used in the several tables that include educational data.

TABLE 4.11. Pattern of presidential voting preference, 1948–1952, in relation to level of education[a]

Level of education	D-D	R-D	O-D[b]	O-R[b]	D-R	R-R
College	11%	16%	10%	17%	17%	24%
High school	46	49	47	49	49	45
Grammar school	43	35	43	34	34	31
	100	100	100	100	100	100
N[c]	(1,856)	(98)	(868)	(904)	(625)	(1,674)

[a] Based on a combination of AIPO 505-TPS, 10-3-52; 506-K, 10-7-52; 507-K, 10-15-52. A few respondents classified as trade-school trainees were excluded from the analysis.

[b] Nonvoters in 1948.

[c] Number of survey respondents in the various categories of prospective voters. If further explanation is needed, see Table 3.12 in preceding chapter.

one way at one election, they may give the college-trained an appearance of political volatility. If they fall in another dimension at the next election, they may make grade-school persons appear to be highly variable. In neither instance does education, as such, necessarily have much bearing on the phenomenon.

Another approach to the question whether switchers are less informed or perhaps less involved than standpatters is to ascertain the relative frequency of "don't know" or "no opinion" answers to policy questions. "No opinion" could probably be translated "respondent doesn't care"; yet generally persons with high levels of information tend to have opinions. If the switchers fitted the theoretical suppositions, we should expect that high proportions of persons with "no opinion" would turn up among switchers in our tabulations. In fact, though, the switchers seem to include no more persons with "no opinion" than do the standpatters of both parties. Rather, they resemble closely in their opinion distribution those groups of standpatters to which they are attracted in the election; or at least they

TABLE 4.12. Patterns of presidential preference, 1948–1952, in relation to distribution of responses to question: "Do you think the U.S. made a mistake in going into the war in Korea or not?"[a]

Response	D-D	R-D	0-D[b]	0-R[b]	D-R	R-R
Yes, mistake	31%	38%	33%	54%	52%	59%
No, not	49	45	44	34	35	28
No opinion	20	17	23	12	13	13
	100	100	100	100	100	100
N	(1,691)	(112)	(676)	(743)	(582)	(1,467)

[a] A consolidation of AIPO 506K, 10-7-52, and 507K, 10-15-52 (as in Table 4.3).
[b] Nonvoters in 1948.

did in the election of 1952 on the issues examined in Tables 4.12 and 4.13, a qualification that may turn out to be important as we proceed. The 1948–52 R-D's tended toward the view that we had not made a mistake in going into Korea but not in quite the same degree as did the standpat Democrats. The 1948–52 D-R's tended toward the view that we had erred but not quite to the same degree as standpat Republicans. In fact, it could be presumed, but not established, from these data, that the policy views of the switchers had a qualitative edge differing from those of the standpatters. Standpat Republicans might respond, in the routine manner of the dedicated partisan, that we (or at least the Truman Administration) had erred in going into Korea; the switcher's view to that effect, though, had been associated with the wrench of desertion of his former candidate and often with a desertion from his party. On the matter of sympathy toward unions or companies in labor disputes (as shown in Table 4.13) switchers included no more indifferents, that is, persons with no opinion, than did the standpatters. Switchers did, though, on this question differ considerably from the standpatters of the party to which

TABLE 4.13. Patterns of presidential preference, 1948–1952, in relation to distribution of responses to question: "In the labor disputes of the last two or three years, have your sympathies, in general, been on the side of the unions or on the side of the companies?"[a]

Response	D-D	R-D	0-D	0-R	D-R	R-R
Unions	62%	49%	57%	33%	34%	20%
Companies	14	25	17	41	36	50
Both	3	6	2	2	3	4
No opinion	21	20	24	24	27	26
	100	100	100	100	100	100
N	(1,687)	(113)	(687)	(748)	(584)	(1,470)

[a] Same surveys as Table 4.12.

they shifted. D-R's were much more disposed to sympathize with unions than were R-R's, a discrepancy mentioned earlier in our discussion of the lack of congruence between the two groups on this question.

An element of the theory of the role of the switchers in providing flexibility for the political system rests on the assumption that they have a low level of interest in politics and that for some reason not entirely apparent they side with the forces of change. Satisfactory measurement of psychological concern about politics requires more elaborate techniques than can readily be used in polls, but the survey data do permit rough differentiation of people according to level of political interest. In several polls in 1952 Gallup interviewers asked: "Generally speaking, how much interest would you say you have in politics—a great deal, a fair amount, only a little, or no interest at all?" Even though it may appear doubtful, many studies demonstrate that self-ratings made by people as they respond to such questions group voters into classes that differ on the average in important respects. Switchers and standpatters are compared with respect to their "interest"

TABLE 4.14. Pattern of presidential preference, 1948–1952, in relation to distribution of responses to question: "Generally speaking, how much interest would you say you have in politics—a great deal, a fair amount, only a little, or no interest at all?"[a]

Response	D-D	R-D	0-D	0-R	D-R	R-R
Great deal	27%	29%	15%	16%	25%	36%
Fair amount	53	49	39	46	57	50
Only a little	17	21	37	31	16	12
None	3	1	9	7	2	2
	100	100	100	100	100	100
N	(2,624)	(126)	(981)	(1,014)	(730)	(1,785)

[a] A combination of AIPO 505-TPS, 10-3-52; 506-K, 10-7-52; 507-K, 10-15-52. Total N for the combined samples, 7,584.

in Table 4.14. The 1948–1952 R-D switchers, though few in number, on the average had about the same interest in politics as the Democratic standpatters. On the other hand, D-R switchers had a somewhat lower level of interest than the Republican standpatters. Of them 25 per cent had "a great deal of interest" in contrast with 36 per cent of the Republican standpatters. Although that difference can hardly be regarded as substantial,[26] the moral may be that under some circumstances those switchers attracted to the winner may express a lesser average interest in politics than the standpatters of the winning party. The large numbers of persons with relatively low interest appear among the nonvoters of 1948—those too young or who did not happen to vote for other reasons. Doubtless a high proportion of these persons did not actually vote, though the chances are that of those who did,

26. If the 1948–1952 D-R group in Table 4.14 had included the same proportion of persons with "a great deal of interest" as the R-R group, about 1 per cent of the total sample would have been re-allocated. It is somewhat difficult to assign to such a small number of voters a role of major importance in producing flexibility or facilitating adjustment in the political system.

the average level of interest fell below the levels of interest of both groups of standpatters and switchers.

Another question about the relation of level of interest to party switching may be put, if we analyze the data in another way. Does gross switching (that is, in both directions, D-R plus R-D) tend to vary with expressed level of interest in politics? The figures indicate that in 1952 there was a slight but irregular relation between gross switching and interest. The percentages switching 1948–1952 in relation to level of interest (with the base N's shown) were as follows:

Great deal of interest	Fair amount	Little	None
16%	19%	20%	16%
(1,410)	(2,447)	(709)	(99)

Apart from the deviance of the "no interest" category, which consisted of few respondents, gross switching rates increased as interest declined. Yet this relation depends to a considerable degree on R-D switches. The rates of switching among 1948 Truman supporters hardly varied with level of interest. The 1948–1952 D-R rates according to level of interest were:

Great deal of interest	Fair amount	Little	None
25%	28%	25%	22%
(727)	(1,490)	(468)	(69)

If one is to trust these data (and doubts are justified), level of interest had no relation to switching from Truman to Eisenhower. And these D-R switchers were the ones who provided the flexibility for the political system. At least the preliminary conclusion may be ventured that in this election involving an exceptionally large voter shift, level of interest really had nothing to do with the adjustment the system made. The suspicion lingers that the relation (or absence of relation) between party switching and level of political interest may be a unique product of the broad characteristics of the particular election observed, a question which can be raised again after the election of 1960 has been examined.

Our manipulations of the data do not establish that party switchers differ materially in level of interest from the standpatters; nor do they establish any role of special significance for those with a low level of interest.[27] Perhaps (and perhaps not) a psychological dimension different from interest was tapped by the 1956 poll question: "How much thought have you given to the coming November election—quite a lot, or only a little?" No profound political truths are likely to emerge from the answers to such a query. Yet we know from everyday observation that the mental anguish dedicated to thought about elections runs from the minimal cerebration of the chap who responds "What election?" to that of the soul-searching of the fellow who feels that he bears on his shoulders the responsibility for deciding the fate of the Republic. The responses to such a question probably divide the population into roughly contrasting categories of people. The upshot of the analysis, though, is that the switchers, in both directions, do not differ materially in the average "thought" they have given the election from the standpatters whom they join, as may be seen from Table 4.15. Slight differences exist in the sample which, even though they actually exist in the total population, are not sufficient in size to excite much concern. Again, too, the

27. The reader should again be reminded that our definition of switching differs from that of the Elmira study from which Berelson drew his theoretical inferences. The behaviors he observed may be concealed in our data.

TABLE 4.15. Patterns of voting preference, 1952–1956, in relation to thought given to election[a]

Thought to election	R-R	D-R	0-R	0-D	R-D	D-D
Quite a lot	59%	52%	29%	34%	54%	56%
Some	21	30	25	23	22	24
Only a little	19	16	36	34	22	18
None	1	2	10	9	2	2
	100	100	100	100	100	100
N	(1,551)	(90)	(547)	(550)	(305)	(902)

[a] A consolidation of AIPO 572K, 10-5-56, and 573K, 10-16-56. The question was: "How much thought have you given to the coming November election—quite a lot, or only a little?"

really marked differences turn up among the "new voters," that is, those who had not voted at the preceding election. In this group those who had given no thought or "only a little" thought to the election were relatively quite numerous.

Still another analysis may give us a faint clue to a peculiar and important characteristic of switchers, though it is not necessarily limited to them. Voters may have feelings of varying intensity about the importance to the country of the election of the candidate they favor. Presumably a willingness to concede that the candidate opposed has his virtues may facilitate the acceptance of the results of elections. In 1944 (as the data of Table 4.16 indicate) switchers had less disposition to regard the election of their candidate as "VERY IMPORTANT to the country" than did standpatters. Relatively more of them thought it merely "better" if their man won or conceded that it would not make much difference to the country which man won. Whether this kind of attitude represented a perceptive judgment of the realities or reflected an underlying psychological peculiarity of the switchers

TABLE 4.16. Presidential preference patterns, 1940–1944, in relation to distribution of judgments about the importance of electing Roosevelt or Dewey[a]

Attitude	D-D	R-D	O-D	O-R	D-R	R-R
Very important to elect Roosevelt	63%	49%	62%	1%	2%	b
Better to elect Roosevelt	33	39	31	1	2	b
Not much difference	3	12	5	7	20	6
Better to elect Dewey	b	—	—	46	32	30
Very important to elect Dewey	b	—	—	40	37	63
Don't know	b	—	2	5	3	b
	100	100	100	100	100	100
N	(852)	(49)	(135)	(100)	(132)	(713)

[a] Based on NORC 30/229, October 1944. The respondent was asked "Which ONE of these ideas comes closest to the way you feel about this election?" He was handed a card containing the following alternatives: 1. It is VERY IMPORTANT to the country that Roosevelt is elected. 2. The country will be better off if Roosevelt is elected. 3. It won't make much difference to the country who is elected. 4. The country will be better off if Dewey is elected. 5. It is VERY IMPORTANT to the country that Dewey is elected. 6. Don't know.

[b] Less than one half of 1 per cent.

one cannot say. A good guess may be that a reserved estimate of the importance of victory may be akin to the tendency of many losing voters to concede, after the election, that the outcome makes far less difference to the country than they were disposed to believe before the election.[28]

We shall revert to this broad question of the character of the switching sector of the electorate after examining the election of 1960; yet at this point some tentative esti-

28. On this point, see V. O. Key, Jr., *Public Opinion and American Democracy* (New York: Knopf, 1961), p. 479.

mates begin to take shape. First, on the basis of the elections examined, it can scarcely be said that party switchers constitute a sector of the electorate significantly lower in political interest than the standpatters. Hence, any general theory of the buffer function in the political system of the uninterested who decide elections and cushion the severity of political conflict by the absorptive capacity of their indifference must either fall or undergo drastic modification.

Instead, the switchers, who (in company with "new" voters) call the turn, are persons whose peculiarity is not lack of interest but agreement on broad political issues with the standpatters toward whom they shift. Democratic defectors diverge markedly in their policy views from Democratic standpatters; Republican renegades likewise depart sharply from the policy views of Republican standpatters. Whether they switch "because" of their policy dissent is another question, but indubitably those who shift to the winning side resemble (on major policy issues of wide concern in the population) the standpatters of that side. This should be regarded as at least a modicum of evidence for the view that those who switch do so to support governmental policies or outlooks with which they agree, not because of subtle psychological or sociological peculiarities.

Another group of voters, though, appears to be markedly different from either the standpatters or the shifters, that is, the "new voters"—those who did not vote at the preceding election, either because they were too young or for some other reason. These persons, on the average, appraise their interest in politics as exceptionally low; they say that, on the average, they give relatively little "thought" to elections. Their voting participation, too, is relatively low, a factor which induces caution about estimates from our pre-election data of their contribution to the outcome of elections.[29] Yet if one were to seek significantly numerous contributors to change, to flexibility, and to adjustment in the political system, he probably should search for them among this category of voters. Their contribution does not derive from their low interest or their indifference, but from the fact that their policy outlooks dilute the standpattism of whichever party resists change and adjustment. Probably this is in large measure the result of the adoption by the young of the dominant outlook of a new day as they move into the party of their fathers.[30]

Such conjectures do not concern the minor flurries of short-term change but focus on the longer-term adjustments which may require some time for their effectuation. As we have seen, the attrition of the electorate (through mortality and the movement of voters into the age brackets of low participation) and the steady infusion of new voters over a few elections bring about fairly substantial changes in the composition of the electorate.[31] The new voters bring with them new outlooks. Thus, in 1940 more new Republicans than R-R's thought there should be more

29. The relatively low participation rates of those of "low" interest as well as of the relatively young has been established by many studies.

30. The new voter group includes large proportions of persons under age 30. The proportions of such persons in the several groups in 1952 (based on a consolidation of AIPO 506 and 507) were as follows: R-R, 12%; D-R, 14%; 0-R, 43%; 0-D, 39%; R-D, 12%; D-D, 13%.

31. These remarks make relevant a comment about the unreality of the conception of the electorate prevalent in most discussions of the role of the switching voter. People ask what group shifts from party to party as if the composition of the electorate remained the same and as if the same persons constituted the swing vote from election to election. That static conception errs, if for no other reason, because of the steady attrition and renewal of the electorate. It errs more gravely from the assumption that in some way or another the same voters—or even the same kinds of voters—would be affected in the same way by the changing tensions as they arise from election to election.

regulation of business (Table 3.12). More new Republicans than standpatters approved the Democratic Administration's farm program (Table 3.13). More new Republicans than standpatters thought the laws governing labor unions were too strict (Table 3.14). In 1952 more new Republicans than R-R's thought that we had not erred in going into Korea (Table 4.12). More new Republicans than standpatters sympathized with unions rather than the companies in the then recent labor disputes (Table 4.13). Perhaps the major adjustments in the political system are induced by this steady renewal which brings persons with a new outlook to the standpatters.[32]

32. All of this is, of course, not inconsistent with the existence within the electorate of a type of voter of low involvement who responds to the stronger of the winds of the moment. And at moments of rather sharp electoral shift the cues of the prevailing wind may be so dominant in the political environment that most of these persons move in the same direction. Yet such persons cannot be regarded as instruments of change and it is doubtful that their number makes their indifference of much significance as an emollient for the friction of change.

CHAPTER 5

DEMOCRATIC RETURN
TO POWER

A great advantage of the stance of the historian may be that as he looks backward events appear far simpler than they seemed to be at the time of their occurrence. Hence, he prudently eschews treatment of the contemporary and pleads for time to gain perspective. On the other hand, some events may be far less simple than others and the perspective of time may create not understanding but opportunity to hoodwink the unwary. In any case, the election of 1960, though it is recent, must be examined. It may turn out in the long run to look simple; yet it certainly differed in important characteristics from the earlier elections we have examined. Additional tools of interpretation will have to be used in describing it.

The skillful exploitation of the events preceding the election of 1960 by the Democratic leadership put the Republican party on the defensive. Yet the terrain the G.O.P. defended could hardly be said to be so clearly unfavorable as that which had been held by the Democrats in 1952. In our external relations, peace of a sort prevailed, though aspects of the foreign situation were disquieting. Castro's revolution in Cuba had led to expropriations of American property and, more seriously, to the conversion of Cuba into a Soviet satellite. The Republican Administration could be charged with having permitted the Soviets to win a bridgehead just off our shores. The inopportune loss of the U-2 reconnaissance plane over Russia had given Khrushchev a pretext for wrecking a scheduled summit meeting with Eisenhower. The inept explanation of the U-2 affair provided grounds for no little criticism of the Administration. Rumblings in the Far East raised the issue whether we should defend Quemoy and Matsu, a point of policy dispute that left the people more confused than involved. On a wider front, debate over the state of the defense apparatus enabled Democrats to make points about the missile gap that seemed telling at the moment, though later perhaps not so well founded. In any case, public appraisal of conflicting claims required judgments, not about things seen or experienced, but about the credibility of disputants who did or did not have access to, or the capacity to judge, facts not known to the public.

Among domestic questions in the last years of the Eisenhower Administration, the state of the economy won most attention. The growth of unemployment presented the issue of government management of the economy in a form somewhat new if not entirely novel. By historical standards employment held at a high level, but now, when the unemployment rate moved a percentage point or so, a million or more persons might be affected.[1] Moreover, the official statistics of unemployment at a given moment, e.g., 6.8 per cent in 1958, understated by far the impact of unemployment. Thus, in October 1958, 17.9 per cent

1. Unemployment as a percentage of the civilian labor force was as follows: 1956, 4.2; 1957, 4.3; 1958, 6.8; 1959, 5.5; 1960, 5.6; and 1961, 6.7.

of all families included in a sample survey reported that they had "had some experience with unemployment during the previous twelve months."[2] Yet, however one measured unemployment, its reduction required arts in governmental management of the economy not commanded by the incumbent Administration or perhaps by any other. In any case, unemployment probably had a far greater political import in 1958—when the Democratic party made exceptionally wide gains—than in 1960, for unemployment dropped in 1959 and 1960. Nevertheless, in some localities exceptionally high rates of unemployment persisted, a circumstance that could be turned to advantage by the Democrats because of Eisenhower's vetoes of bills to initiate special measures for the relief of depressed areas.

The state of the domestic economy became intertwined, as everything now seemed to, with the Communist-capitalist rivalry. The comparative rates of Soviet and American economic growth generated a large volume of political discourse in 1960 and earlier. High rates of Russian growth were said to lend substance to Khrushchev's threat to "bury" us, though the extrapolation of rates of growth from their 1960 points of departure put the date of the funeral a considerable time in the future.

Other long-standing issues precipitated maneuvers, proposals for action, and disputes about action, though how extensively people concerned themselves with these issues cannot be said. These matters usually turned up as conflicts between the Democratic Congress and Eisenhower,

2. Eva Mueller and Jay Schmiedeskamp, *Persistent Unemployment, 1957–1961* (Kalamazoo: Upjohn Institute for Employment Research, 1962), p. 7. In a June 1958 survey, 5.1 per cent of the heads of families were unemployed at the time; another 8.0 per cent had been unemployed at one time or another within the preceding twelve months. In 8.1 per cent of the families some member of the family was working fewer hours than usual.

and their outcomes probably on the whole helped to build a picture of the Republican party as a party not genuinely enthusiastic about federal aid to education and not dedicated to the raising of the statutory minimum wage. In other areas—such as civil rights and medical care—the apportionment of credit and blame between the parties had to be even more ambiguous, but Eisenhower scarcely embraced the opportunity to tie the groups concerned to the G.O.P. by vigorous advocacy of their cause.

A recitation of the calendar of events preceding an election does not necessarily give us a satisfactory picture of the world to which voters react as they cast their ballots. Such an account, no matter how accurate or complete it may be, tells us directly nothing about the impressions of the march of affairs that exist in the minds of the voters. Differences in voters' interest, in their range of information, in the orientation of their attention, in their first-hand experience, and in their exposure to communications produce enormous variation in their perceptions of events and, consequently, in their appraisals of the alternatives posed by the electoral system. The explanation of voting behavior requires estimation of the modal parameters of the perceptions of the political world to which voters respond, a task to which insufficient resources have been devoted.[3]

The nature of voter perception of the political world gains import when we recall the earlier discussion of the resemblance of the electoral system to an echo chamber. Voters respond to what they see and hear; the nature of their response depends upon what they see and hear

3. The most thorough efforts are based on analyses of free answers to open ended questions put by the Survey Research Center. See Angus Campbell, P. E. Converse, W. E. Miller, and D. E. Stokes, *The American Voter* (New York: Wiley, 1960).

(which, in turn, is conditioned by what is in their heads to begin with). Points of political leadership and of communication of political intelligence, by influencing what people see and hear, fix the range of voter response (within the limits of the situation as shaped by the irrepressible flow of events) as they transmit information to the electorate. What did voters see and hear as the election of 1960 approached? If we had satisfactory data on that point, we could get along with fewer words. Nevertheless, contrasts with earlier campaign situations make plausible the supposition that voters with even the slightest attention to affairs political saw a political landscape with broad peculiarities differentiating it in its general aspects from earlier campaign situations.

The year 1960 certainly did not resemble 1932, when conditions of economic disaster prevailed, Democrats could saddle the "ins" with responsibility for all of many discontents, and the Republicans could scarcely command a respectful hearing for their defense. Nor could 1960 be said to be another 1936 when Roosevelt in his final speech of the campaign in Madison Square Garden spoke of the "old enemies," "business and financial monopoly, speculation, reckless banking, class antagonism." Never, he said to the vengeful roar of the crowd, had these forces been so united against a candidate and "I welcome their hatred." "I should like to have it said of my first Administration that in it the forces of selfishness and of lust for power met their match. I should like to have it said of my second Administration that in it these forces met their master." The campaign and the preceding events made it seem as if the stakes of the game were both real and high—and they were. Nor is it probable that 1960 in the minds of voters resembled 1952, when a lack of confidence in the incumbent Administration clearly permeated a large sector of the electorate—and when the Republican candidate appeared to many voters as the sure solvent of their anxieties.

The political world of 1960 had its ambiguities which surely must have become even more ambiguous as they seeped through the communications system to take shape in the minds of the voters. What did the voters see? They certainly saw two candidates, neither of whom had been tested in the presidential role. Neither could point to a record of performance as could Roosevelt in 1940 or Eisenhower in 1956. Neither could claim to be more than an unknown quantity as presidential timber, though Mr. Nixon made the most of his conspicuous performance of the vice-presidential chores. The television debates made the candidates visible to the viewing public in disputation, yet, despite the extravagant claims of the TV network managers, the "great" debates, tailored to the requisites of show business, did not enable the candidates to develop their positions on the questions confronting the country. As debates, these affairs hovered at a level somewhere in the neighborhood of bush-league college debates. The TV screen conveyed not much more than an impression of the relative glibness, composure under fire, capacity in repartee, and quickness of wit of the contenders. Nor does the deadly eye of the TV camera, as some telecasters claim, unerringly search out the inner strengths and weaknesses of character of those upon whom it is focused.[4]

If most voters saw one or two or three great and overriding considerations as salient, they must surely have seen them far less distinctly than they did in 1936 or 1952. Specific policy questions doubtless had clarity

4. For discussions of the debates, see *The Great Debates*, ed. Sidney Kraus (Bloomington: Indiana University Press, 1962).

for the relatively small sectors of the electorate directly involved or concerned, yet the campaign could not have been perceived by many people as a great and blunt confrontation of special privilege and mass welfare as 1936 must have been seen. Voters, rather, saw candidates who expressed agreement on many basic propositions. Said Vice President Nixon in the first debate: "I agree with Senator Kennedy completely on that score. Where we disagree is in the means that we would use to get the most out of our economy." Senator Kennedy wanted to get this great country on the move; Vice President Nixon could not disagree with that sentiment, but he wanted to get things in motion in a less costly manner—and he could not very well concede that the country was in a state of complete paralysis anyway.

In brief, the political world must have seemed far more ambiguous to most people in 1960 than it had in such campaigns as 1936, 1940, or 1952. The candidates were, on their record, personable ciphers. Their broad objectives often sounded similar. When they differed, often they differed about matters both remote and complex. Moreover, in special degree, voters had to concern themselves with future probabilities rather than with past performance, and the average voter, like the rest of us, does not perceive a future extruded with crystalline clarity from the chaos of current ambiguity. Even the press did not simplify matters as it had in 1952 and 1956, when the citizen found no encouragement to indecision in the media which stood as a monolith in support of Eisenhower. In 1960 the commentators, editors, and reporters were, if not themselves befuddled, divided.

Engulfed by a campaign fallout composed chiefly of fluffy and foggy political stimuli, the voter tends to let himself be guided by underlying and durable identifications, group loyalties, and preferences rather than by the meaningless and fuzzy buzz of the transient moment. In every campaign, of course, these underlying identifications and loyalties provide cues for action for many voters, perhaps many more than a majority. Yet in 1960 the electorate, or most of it, seemed to be compelled to rely in especial degree upon these basic attitudes and identifications; about the only clear-cut aspects of the appeals of the campaign related to basic identifications with one group or another.

The 1960 election results are not easy to place in any coherent pattern.* Yet even in their superficial aspects the returns differed markedly from those of most recent presidential elections. Aside from the highly important fact that the 1960 balloting brought the first Democratic presidential victory since 1948, for the first time since 1936 the Democratic party increased its proportion of the vote over its showing at the previous presidential election. The net shift in the vote—nearly 8 per cent—was the largest since 1928-1932; and, although no single overriding issue of public policy came to the fore, the involvement of the electorate was high. Between 1956 and 1960 the total vote increased by 11 per cent, with the most marked gain in the South. In the nation as a whole, 64.3 per cent of the potentially eligible electorate (persons of voting age) went to the polls—a proportionate turnout even higher than that in the highly charged electoral contest of 1952.[5]

---

* Editor's note: Narrative by V. O. Key, Jr., stops here. The rest of this chapter, except for a page or so which Key wrote and which is inserted later with suitable notice, is supplied by the editor, who attempted to follow lines which Key apparently had in mind. All the tables in the chapter were prepared by Key.

5. P. E. Converse, A. Campbell, W. E. Miller, and D. E. Stokes,

The 1960 results differed from most other recent elections in other respects as well. Unlike most successful presidential nominees, John F. Kennedy ran substantially behind his party's congressional ticket and behind most other Democratic office seekers. His popular-vote margin over Richard M. Nixon was exceptionally narrow.[6] And, for the first time since 1928, Kennedy's Roman Catholic faith made the religion of one of the presidential candidates a major preoccupation of the campaign. As virtually every account of the election noted, the impact of this religious issue left a marked imprint on the returns.

The large net shift in the vote between 1956 and 1960 was accompanied by an even larger number of switches from one party to the other by individual voters. Of persons who voted in both elections, probably more than one in five switched parties at the presidential level between 1956 and 1960. The movements from Republican to Democratic and vice versa are shown for a variety of categories of voters by Table 5.1. Although the dominant tide in most groups was to the Democratic party, in most groups there was substantial switching in both directions.

There were also marked differences in the kinds of groups where each party's losses were heaviest. The Republicans lost supporters in every status group, but their proportionate losses were heaviest among the lower-status groups: the skilled and unskilled workers in the analysis by occupation, and persons who did not attend college in

"Stability and Change in 1960: A Reinstating Election," *American Political Science Review*, 55 (1961), 269. The proportion of estimated adults over 21 who voted in 1952 was 62.7 per cent.

6. In the nation as a whole, Kennedy's share of the two-party presidential vote was about 4.7 percentage points below the share of the national congressional vote polled by Democratic House candidates. Kennedy's popular-vote margin over Nixon was 118,550, in a total presidential vote of 68,838,979. *America Votes*, ed. Richard M. Scammon, vol. 4 (Pittsburgh: University of Pittsburgh Press, 1962).

TABLE 5.1. Switches in presidential voting preference, 1956–1960, within groups with specified social and demographic characteristics[a]

Group	% of 1956 R's, R-D		% of 1956 D's, D-R		% of new voters, D	
Occupation						
Business and professional	22	(965)	15	(368)	39	(194)
White-collar	18	(522)	8	(244)	56	(137)
Skilled	36	(734)	12	(488)	58	(239)
Unskilled	39	(690)	7	(590)	68	(383)
Farmers and farm laborers	26	(460)	7	(217)	66	(96)
Education						
Grammar school	31	(1,121)	11	(840)	63	(881)
High school	30	(1,730)	9	(988)	59	(971)
College	19	(897)	19	(258)	52	(335)
Religion						
Protestant	17	(2,860)	17	(1,200)	53	(1,647)
Catholic	59	(901)	4	(684)	81	(458)
Jewish	28	(57)	1	(208)	92	(38)
Race						
White	26	(3,791)	10	(1,978)	56	(1,733)
Negro	44	(182)	12	(239)	71	(482)

[a] A consolidation of AIPO 635-K, 9-7-60; 636-K, 9-26-60; and 637-K, 10-18-60. As earlier, a number in parentheses (N) is the number of respondents on which the percentage is based. If any further clarification of this is needed at this point, see the note to Table 4.1.

the analysis by education. In some of these lower-status groups the shift to Kennedy was very large. Thus, among unskilled workers who had voted Republican in 1956, close to four in every ten reported an intention to switch Democratic in 1960.

This 1956–1960 Republican attrition along status lines was reversed among 1956 Democratic voters. Among them there was some tendency for the high-status groups—the college graduates and members of the business and professional occupational category—to have the highest proportions of deserters of the Democratic cause. Even when allowances are made for variations in the size of the different status groups covered by the data in Table 5.1, it is clear that between 1956 and 1960 the status polarization of the American electorate sharpened.

New voters who came into the active electorate in 1960 were apparently no more likely to vote for Kennedy than were those who voted at both elections, a finding that emphasizes still further the importance for the 1960 outcome of the decisions made by the switching voters.[7] Had the new voters been substantially more pro-Kennedy than persons who voted both in 1956 and in 1960, this would account for part of the sharp increase in Democratic strength in 1960. As it was, however, in order to win his slender margin of victory, Kennedy had to record large net gains for the Democratic party among the same voters who in 1956 had given President Eisenhower a landslide victory.

A substantial number of Negroes who had voted for Eisenhower in 1956 shifted to Kennedy; and the proportion of Negroes who shifted Democratic between 1956 and 1960 clearly outnumbered the proportion of Negroes shifting the other way. Yet the increase in the Democratic percentage among Negroes differed very little from the increase in the Democratic percentage in the electorate as a whole, and much of whatever special advantage the heavy Democratic Negro vote gave Kennedy in 1960 had to come from the concentration of Negroes in close and important states and from a rise in the total number of Negro votes cast.

7. In their study of the 1960 voting, the Survey Research Center of the University of Michigan also found that the two-party vote division among new voters differed "only negligibly" from that of the nation as a whole. P. E. Converse et al., "Stability and Change in 1960," pp. 271-272.

It is, however, the data on the voters' religion that reveal the most dramatic contrasts in the rates of vote-switching between 1956 and 1960. Jewish voters, who had been overwhelmingly for Stevenson in 1956, remained overwhelmingly for Kennedy in 1960, in part, perhaps, because Richard Nixon was not wildly popular in the American Jewish community. Protestants and Catholics, however, differed markedly in the way they switched from one party to the other. Events quickly brought the religious question to the surface in the 1960 campaign. On September 7 a group of Protestant churchmen headed by the Reverend Norman Vincent Peale issued a public statement questioning the wisdom of choosing any man of the Roman Catholic faith for president.[8] On September 12, Kennedy appeared before the Greater Houston Ministerial Association in Houston, Texas, to discuss his religion and its bearing upon his fitness to serve as president. Many of the questions from the ministers who gathered to hear him reflected intense Protestant concern over having a Catholic president.[9]

This concern over the religious issue was widely distributed throughout the American electorate. In pre-election interviews conducted with prospective voters for the Survey Research Center of the University of Michigan, nearly 40 per cent of the sample voluntarily introduced the subject of Kennedy's religion before any direct probing was initiated by the interviewer.[10] And, as the data in Table 5.1 indicate, there was a sharp divergence between the way Protestants and Catholics responded to the alternatives presented them by the campaign.

8. *New York Times,* Sept. 8, 1960, p. 1.
9. Theodore H. White, *The Making of the President 1960* (New York: Atheneum, 1961), pp. 260-262.
10. P. E. Converse *et al.,* "Stability and Change in 1960," p. 276.

There were Protestants who switched from Eisenhower to Kennedy between 1956 and 1960, but these gains were counterbalanced by a sizable group of defections among Protestants who had voted Democratic in 1956 but who refused to support Kennedy in 1960. Other data indicate that from 1956–1960 there was almost no net change at all in the Democratic percentage of the Protestant vote, despite the fact that the electorate as a whole was nearly 8 per cent more Democratic in 1960 than in 1956.[11] Except for 1956, the 1960 election undoubtedly brought forth the poorest Democratic showing among Protestants since the Democratic party became the normal majority party of the United States following the Great Depression.

Nevertheless, Kennedy's election was still possible because among Catholics there was a massive movement to the Democratic party. Of the Catholics who had voted for Eisenhower in 1956, close to six in every ten shifted to Kennedy in 1960. Very few Catholic voters who had supported Stevenson deserted Kennedy four years later. The net effect of this shifting to and fro among Catholics, other data indicate, was to raise the Democratic share of the votes of Catholics from about 50 per cent in 1956 to about 80 per cent in 1960.[12]

These differences between the way Protestants and Catholics responded to the campaign alternatives presented them in 1956 and 1960 find added reflection in Table 5.2. The switchers from Democratic to Republican, like the R-R's and the new voters who were drawn to the Republican banner, were an overwhelmingly Protestant group. But a very sizable proportion of the new Demo-

11. The Survey Research Center reported that Eisenhower won 64 per cent of the "Protestant vote" in 1956 and that Nixon won 63 per cent in 1960. *Ibid.*, p. 272.
12. *Ibid.*, pp. 272-273.

TABLE 5.2. Patterns of presidential voting, 1956–1960, in relation to religious affiliation[a]

Affiliation	D-D	R-D	0-D[b]	0-R[b]	D-R	R-R
Protestant	59%	40%	51%	81%	81%	88%
Roman Catholic	30	56	42	11	7	7
Jewish	7	1	3	2	2	c
Other	3	c	3	5	7	2
None	1	3	1	1	3	2
No answer	—	—	—	—	—	1
	100	100	100	100	100	100
N	(612)	(321)	(154)	(147)	(84)	(840)

[a] AIPO 638-K, 11-15-60.
[b] Nonvoters in 1956.
[c] Less than one half of 1 per cent.

cratic voters were Catholics; and the R-D group, which played such an important role in the final outcome of the election, was more than half Catholic. The religious affiliation of the standpat Republican and the standpat Democratic groups also differed sharply. The proportion of consistent Republican voters who were Catholics (7 per cent) was very small. The odds are that the appeal to Catholic group loyalties mounted by the nomination of Kennedy reduced the cadre of Catholic Republicans to its hard core. But of standpat Democrats in 1956 and 1960, three in ten were Catholics. The data in Table 5.2 underscore the large contribution Catholics made to Democratic voting strength even in the Eisenhower landslide year of 1956.

Both loyalties and antagonisms aroused by Kennedy's Roman Catholic religious faith had a powerful impact on the voters' response to the 1960 campaign. Yet, large as the American Roman Catholic population was, had the election been converted into a religious census, Vice President Nixon, rather than Senator Kennedy, would have been elected president in 1960. There were also other group loyalties that could potentially be activated, and Kennedy tried hard to appeal to them in his campaign. Throughout the campaign the Democratic presidential nominee referred repeatedly to the theme of party loyalty. At a campaign strategy meeting with his closest advisers, it was decided that he should "make clear that the two parties were wholly different in goals and pin the Republican label on Nixon as tightly as possible, hammering him as the spiritual descendant of McKinley, Harding, Hoover, Landon, and Dewey."[13] Nixon, by contrast, took a different tack. As Stanley Kelley puts it: "Vice President Nixon tried to induce the voter to make a choice between men. Senator Kennedy strove to make his choice one between parties as well as candidates."[14]

Both candidates had good reason to adopt the campaign stance they selected: there were in 1960 a good many more Democrats than Republicans. But Kennedy had a special need to sound the call for party loyalty. Among a majority of Roman Catholics, party loyalty, predominantly Democratic, would reinforce the attraction of having a co-religionist at the head of the Democratic presidential ticket. In any event it was probably clear from the start that Kennedy was going to get the lion's share of the "Catholic vote." But party loyalty was for Kennedy, among Protestant Democrats, a potential antidote to the anti-Catholicism that the emotions of the campaign were arousing. By appealing to party loyalty Kennedy might hope to rally many Democrats who might otherwise be lost to him on the religious issue. The net

13. White, *Making of President 1960*, p. 321.
14. Stanley Kelley, Jr., "The Presidential Campaign," in *The Presidential Election and Transition 1960–1961*, ed. Paul T. David (Washington: Brookings Institution, 1961), p. 65.

effect of Kennedy's campaign strategy was to try to use party loyalty to supersede religious antagonism among Protestant Democrats.

An indication of how well Kennedy succeeded in rallying Democratic sympathizers to his cause appears in Table 5.3. New voters who considered themselves Democrats

TABLE 5.3. Switching in presidential voting preference, 1956–1960, in relation to party identification[a]

1960 identi- fication	% of 1956 D's, D-R	% of 1956 R's, R-D	% of new voters, D
Republican	100 (20)	4 (619)	17 (176)
Democratic	4 (606)	78 (287)	86 (369)
Independent	14 (105)	32 (280)	57 (205)

[a] AIPO 637-K, 10-18-60. The form of the question was: "In politics, as of TODAY, do you consider yourself a Republican, Democrat, or Independent?" Following is an illustration of how to use this table. The figures "14 (105)" at the bottom of the first column mean that 105 people interviewed in October 1960 said they considered themselves Independents and recalled voting for Stevenson in 1956, and that 14 per cent of these people said they were going to vote for Nixon in 1960.

voted overwhelmingly for Kennedy; Republican new voters voted almost as strongly for Nixon. Among those who voted in both elections, Kennedy pulled very few 1956 Republican voters who considered themselves Republicans in 1960. But he also lost relatively few (4 per cent) of the 1960 Democratic identifiers who had voted Democratic in 1956. And of the sizable group of persons who considered themselves Democrats in 1960 but who had supported Eisenhower in 1956, close to eight in ten planned to vote for Kennedy in 1960.

This massive shift among 1960 Democratic identifiers takes on added interest when it is compared with the magnitude of the shift to Kennedy among 1956 Catholic Republican voters, a shift pinpointed by the data in Table

5.1. That table, it will be recalled, suggested that about three fifths of the 1956 Catholic Republican voters shifted to Kennedy in 1960. Among persons who had voted for Eisenhower in 1956, the proportion of individuals who in 1960 regarded themselves as Democrats who switched to Kennedy was substantially larger than the proportion of Catholics who came to Kennedy's support.[15]

One must be wary of attributing this remarkable shift among Democrats to the eloquence of the Kennedy oratory or to the efficacy of his campaign tactics. Kennedy was, after all, running against Richard Nixon, not President Eisenhower. Part of the shift may have occurred because Nixon was unable to match the nonpartisan, above-politics appeal of President Eisenhower. There also remained many Democrats who had been for Eisenhower whom Kennedy was unable to win, and others who had supported Stevenson whom he lost. Nevertheless, amid the millions of switchers from one party to the other between 1956 and 1960, a major trend toward Kennedy developed among Democratic party identifiers who were returning to the fold.

Some insight into the motives underpinning this shift emerges from the voters' response to another question asked by the Gallup poll in 1960: "Looking ahead for the next few years, which political party—the Republican or the Democratic—do you think will be best for people like yourself?" The phrase "people like yourself" could undoubtedly mean different things to different people. It could be interpreted to mean people of your race; it could

---

15. A sizable portion of these 1960 Democratic identifiers who had voted for Eisenhower, of course, were Catholics. The odds are that Kennedy got an overwhelming vote among Catholics who considered themselves Democrats but had voted for Eisenhower. Among Protestant Democrats who had backed Eisenhower, the shift to Kennedy, though still large, was undoubtedly much smaller.

mean people of your social class or income bracket; it could mean people of your religious faith. Nevertheless, the question was aimed at the link between party preference and the voters' self-identification; and, as the data in Table 5.4 indicate, the relation between the way voters responded to the question and their vote intention was very strong.

TABLE 5.4. Switching in presidential preference, 1956–1960, in relation to response to question: "Looking ahead for the next few years, which political party—the Republican or the Democratic—do you think will be best for people like yourself?"[a]

Response	% of 1956 D's, D-R	% of 1956 R's, R-D	% of new voters, D
Republican	83 (30)	3 (741)	10 (185)
Democratic	5 (527)	70 (339)	88 (375)
No difference	43 (51)	33 (135)	45 (68)
No opinion	48 (27)	43 (53)	42 (43)

[a] AIPO 635-K, 9-7-60. Total N, 2907.

Those whose opinion on the question and previous vote were congruent remained in high degree with the party they had supported previously. There were very few 1956 Democratic voters who in 1960 felt the Republican party would be better for people like themselves, but among those who did hold this view, the shift to the Republican party was strong. On the other hand, there was a sizable group of 1956 Eisenhower voters—about an eighth of all those holding a preference—who in 1960 felt that the Democratic party would be better for people like themselves. Of them, seven in ten shifted to Mr. Kennedy. The voting decisions of new voters also demonstrated a strong relation to their response to the question. Among voters who expressed a preference for one party or the other, more favored the Democratic party than favored the

G.O.P. The data thus suggest that in 1960, group loyalties other than religion were on balance working to Mr. Kennedy's advantage.

Examination of the voters' party loyalties, religious loyalties, and self-identified group loyalties goes some way toward explaining the broad contours of the 1960 vote. Yet even in 1960 most individuals who ended up in the respective party columns tended to hold policy views appropriate to their party choice. Those who switched parties between 1956 and 1960 also tended to shift in a manner that was consistent with their policy views.

As the campaign moved toward its climax, Dr. Gallup again asked the question on which the Republican party had held an edge throughout the 1950's: "Which political party do you think would be more likely to keep the United States out of World War III—the Republican party or the Democratic party?" The responses, which are detailed in Table 5.5, indicated that the Republican party still led the Democrats on this question, though not by as wide a margin as the G.O.P. had enjoyed in 1956. The new voters' policy positions were congruent with their

TABLE 5.5. Switching in presidential voting preference, 1956–1960, in relation to response to question: "Which political party do you think would be more likely to keep the United States out of World War III—the Republican party or the Democratic party?"[a]

Response	% of 1956 D's, D-R	% of 1956 R's, R-D	% of new voters, D
Republican	42 (88)	6 (758)	28 (242)
Democratic	3 (309)	91 (163)	90 (233)
Same	4 (239)	50 (153)	64 (171)
No opinion	6 (103)	61 (120)	68 (114)

[a] AIPO 637-K, 10-18-60.

vote intention to a quite high degree, and a sizable percentage of 1956 Democratic voters who believed in 1960 that the Republicans would be better able to keep the country out of another war switched Republican. On the other hand, there was a sizable bloc of voters who had supported Eisenhower in 1956 who favored the Democratic party on the war-peace issue in 1960, and nine of every ten of these voters reported they intended to switch to Senator Kennedy.

Had only those persons voted who felt that one party or the other was better equipped to keep the peace, Mr. Nixon, rather than Mr. Kennedy, would probably have been elected president in 1960.[16] But the Democrats made up for this disadvantage—enough to avert defeat—among the large group of voters who felt that the prospects for continued peace would be the same under either party and among those who had no opinion on the question. Very few 1956 Democratic voters who felt that the prospects for peace would be the same under either party in 1960 left the Democratic party in 1960; but half the 1956 Republican voters who in 1960 felt the Democrats would be equally as good as the Republicans in avoiding World War III moved to Mr. Kennedy's support. New voters who believed that the parties would be equally good at maintaining peace or had no opinion also broke heavily for Kennedy. Among those who felt that the choice between the parties on the basic issue of war or peace was at least a standoff, other factors seemed to be exerting a strong pull toward the Democratic party. This, in addition to the slackening since 1956 of the advantage the Republicans enjoyed on the issue, probably helped

16. Among those who felt that one party or the other would be more likely to keep the United States out of World War III, 54.1 per cent reported that they intended to vote for Nixon.

make it possible for Mr. Kennedy to win his narrow victory.

Other issue considerations, however, were working to the Democrats' advantage. Of those who had a preference on the question, "Looking ahead for the next few years, which political party—the Republican or the Democratic —do you think will do the best job of keeping the country prosperous?" about three preferred the Democrats for every two who gave the edge to the Republicans. These data, found in Table 5.6, take on added interest when they are compared with the response the identical question elicited when it was put to the voters in 1956 (Table 4.9). In 1956, it will be recalled, the Republican and Democratic parties stood about even on this question in the population generally—probably the highest expression of public confidence in the Republicans' ability to avoid another depression in any election campaign since 1929. But by 1960 this confidence had again waned, and the Democratic nominee enjoyed a clear-cut advantage on the question of which party could better maintain prosperity.

TABLE 5.6. Switching in presidential voting preference, 1956–1960, in relation to response to question: "Looking ahead for the next few years, which political party—the Republican or the Democratic—do you think will do the best job of keeping the country prosperous?"[a]

Response	% of 1956 D's, D-R		% of 1956 R's, R-D		% of new voters, D	
Republican	85	(27)	3	(673)	18	(195)
Democratic	3	(609)	86	(280)	90	(399)
Same	8	(57)	31	(104)	46	(56)
No opinion	29	(41)	39	(124)	45	(109)

[a] AIPO 637-K, 10-18-60. Total N, 2,993.

In 1960, at least, more people also tended to prefer one party or the other on this question than on the question about which party was better equipped to keep the peace.[17] And the relationship between the voters' response to the domestic prosperity question and their vote was strong, both for new voters and for those who voted both in 1956 and in 1960. The number of 1956 Democratic voters who in 1960 thought the Republicans would do better at preserving prosperity was very small, but nearly all of them switched Republican. And among the large group of 1956 Republican voters who in 1960 felt the Democrats would do a better job of keeping prosperity, there was a major shift to the Democratic party. In the group who thought the ability of the two parties to cope with the problem was the same, there was on balance a net movement to the Democrats.

Further evidence of the congruence between voters' policy views on the prosperity question and the party they intended to support in the presidential contest appears in Table 5.7. Standpat Democrats backed their party on the issue almost to a man, while an overwhelming majority of the Republican standpatters took the contrary view. Voters who shifted to the Democratic party between 1956 and 1960 and the new voters who intended to support the Democratic nominee also heavily endorsed the Democratic party on the prosperity issue; and the new voters

17. The proportion of respondents who expressed a preference for one party or the other on the domestic prosperity question was 81.7 per cent; on the war-peace question it was 66.6 per cent. Although the "no opinion" rate was slightly higher on the war-peace question, most of the difference stemmed from the fact that substantially more persons felt that the two parties would do equally well on keeping the peace than considered them equal on the domestic prosperity problem. The proportions who said the performance of the parties would be the same were: maintain domestic prosperity, 8.1 per cent; avoid World War III, 20.9 per cent.

TABLE 5.7. Patterns of presidential voting and preference, 1956–1960, in relation to response to question: "Looking ahead for the next few years, which political party—the Republican or the Democratic—do you think will do the best job of keeping the country prosperous?"[a]

Response	D-D	R-D	0-D	0-R	D-R	R-R
Republican	1%	6%	8%	55%	38%	78%
Democrat	87	71	77	14	34	5
Same	8	9	5	10	8	8
No opinion	4	14	10	21	20	9
	100	100	100	100	100	100
N	(673)	(340)	(469)	(290)	(61)	(841)

[a] AIPO 637-K, 10-18-60. Total N, 2897.

who rallied to the Republican side tended to favor the G.O.P. on the issue—though considerably less strongly than the R-R's. The number of respondents who shifted from Democratic to Republican is so small as to cast some doubt on the figures; but among those who did turn up in Dr. Gallup's sample, there was very weak support for the Republican party on the prosperity issue. The figures thus create at least a suspicion that Mr. Nixon was pulling to his support some people who were less than enthusiastic about the G.O.P.'s economic policies, a point to which we shall return later.

As we have seen, among members of the Gallup poll's sample in 1960 the correlations between vote intention and opinions on the respective abilities of the two parties to maintain prosperity and avoid World War III were high. The attitudes tapped by those questions undoubtedly were important—even in an election year when for an unusually large number of voters the policy differences between the two presidential nominees may have seemed ambiguous. However, one still has no assurance that those were the issues that were uppermost in all, or most, voters' minds as they came to a decision in the presidential contest. A voter could feel that the Democratic party was more likely to be successful in maintaining prosperity, or that the G.O.P. was the best bet to avoid World War III, and yet be more concerned with some other issue of public policy. One question asked by Dr. Gallup's interviewers, however, did try to get at what the voters themselves perceived as the major problems before the country. It was worded: "What do you think is the MOST important problem facing this country today?" The following were the problems cited most frequently by respondents who at the time of interview had decided on their presidential choice, and the percentage of such respondents who mentioned each problem:[18]

Foreign policy and defense policy

Threat of war, general	18%
Foreign relations, communicating, understanding, getting along with other people and nations	18
Our relations with Russia (no mention of war threat)	9
Threat of Communism, threat of Communist countries other than Russia	8
Cuba, Castro, etc.	7
Threat of war with Russia	5
Problems of defense, atomic warfare, U.S. military strength lag, preparedness	5

18. $N = 2,816$. AIPO 637-K, 10-16-60. Certain other problems that are not listed above, such as "juvenile delinquency and teen-age problems," were mentioned by smaller numbers of respondents. The percentages for the problems that are listed do not add to 100.

DOMESTIC POLICY

Domestic economic problems, inflation, higher prices, etc.	12%
Unemployment	7
Racial problems, segregation, integration, discrimination	6
Education problems, crowded buildings, fewer teachers, and low pay	2

Although a generalized concern over foreign-policy problems and the maintenance of peace was certainly widespread in 1960, it was probably not so strong a factor pushing voters toward one party as foreign-policy concerns had been in 1952. Among voters who cited foreign-policy considerations, the difference between the number of persons who supported Nixon and the number for Kennedy was fairly small. Nor was any single domestic problem dominant in the public mind in 1960.

There were also some notable omissions from this listing by prospective voters of the "most important" problems facing the country in 1960. In the midst of a campaign in which Democratic orators made frequent charges that American prestige had slipped seriously under the Eisenhower Administration, it is worth noting that the state of American prestige abroad was cited by less than one per cent of the voting population. Farm policy was mentioned by one per cent of those interviewed, and social security and medicare together by less than one half of one per cent. Domestic economic policy and unemployment, on the other hand, received a good deal more emphasis; and close to one American in every five put those issues above even war or peace and relations with the Communist world.

A detailed inspection of the poll results indicates that those voters who cited the threat of war and problems of getting along with other nations gave a slight edge to Nixon. Yet among voters who cited most other foreign-policy concerns, Nixon and Kennedy were about even; and the problem of defense and preparedness apparently was a Democratic argument. The smaller number of prospective voters who were preoccupied with domestic problems, however, were strongly for Kennedy. Those who cited domestic economic policy or racial problems (which included discrimination) reported by two to one that they intended to vote for Kennedy. Among the tiny number of respondents who cited education, Kennedy's edge was roughly three to one, and among those especially concerned with unemployment, Kennedy led Nixon by five to one.

After getting prospective voters to list what they regarded as the most important problem before the country, the Gallup poll's interviewers then asked them which party would be better able to handle that problem. As the data in Table 5.8 make clear, there was a very strong relationship between the voters' response to this question and their vote intentions in the Kennedy-Nixon presidential contest. Voters who felt that the party they had voted for in 1956 was best able to handle the most important problem before the country in 1960 remained, in extraordinarily high degree, with the party they had supported in 1956. But voters whose assessment of which party was best equipped to handle the "most important" issue of 1960 was inconsistent with their 1956 vote tended overwhelmingly to cast a vote in 1960 that was in line with their 1960 policy position. The number of 1956 Democrats who were inconsistent in this manner is small; but the number of 1956 Republican voters who found

TABLE 5.8. Switching in presidential voting preference, 1956–1960, in relation to response to question: "Which political party do you think can do a better job of handling the problem (the MOST important problem facing this country) you have just mentioned—the Republican party or the Democratic party?"[a]

Response	% of 1956 D's, D-R	% of 1956 R's, R-D	% of new voters, D
Republican	89 (36)	2 (708)	17 (198)
Democratic	1 (545)	96 (228)	93 (326)
No difference	12 (103)	40 (146)	50 (97)
No opinion	5 (36)	43 (97)	55 (117)

[a] AIPO 637-K, 10-16-60. The question had been preceded by the inquiry: "What do you think is the MOST important problem facing this country today?"

themselves in this inconsistent position was much larger, and of them, 96 per cent switched to Kennedy. New voters also broke heavily for the party they favored on their most important issue; and once again those who felt it unlikely that there would be much difference between the parties on the issue or had no opinion tended to be pulled with the dominant electoral tide to the Democratic party.

This relationship between the voters' assessment of which party could best handle the most important problem before the country and their presidential preference is also illuminated by the data in Table 5.9. Both the Republican standpatters and the Democratic standpatters strongly endorsed the party whose presidential nominee they supported in 1956 and 1960. New voters also tended to resemble the group to whose support they moved far more than did any group that voted for the opposite party. Nevertheless, the peculiarities of the data on the D-R's arouse additional curiosity. We have already seen (in Table 5.7) that this group gave only the most grudging endorsement of the G.O.P.'s capacity to maintain pros-

TABLE 5.9. Patterns of presidential preference, 1956–1960, in relation to response to question: "Which political party do you think can do a better job of handling the problem (the MOST important problem facing this country) you have just mentioned—the Republican party or the Democratic party?"[a]

Response	D-D	R-D	0-D	0-R	D-R	R-R
Republican	1%	5%	7%	56%	52%	81%
Democratic	79	63	65	8	12	1
No difference	13	17	10	16	20	10
No opinion	5	12	14	17	3	7
No answer	2	3	4	3	13	1
	100	100	100	100	100	100
N	(678)	(348)	(469)	(298)	(61)	(850)

[a] AIPO 637-K, 10-16-60. The question had been preceded by the inquiry: "What do you think is the MOST important problem facing this country today?" Total N, 2,993.

perity. Apparently they were somewhat more likely to feel that the Republicans would be better able to cope with the problem that they regarded as most important— or at least to feel that there would be no difference between the parties on that score. Even so, their expression of confidence in the G.O.P was lukewarm: just over half felt that the Republican party was better equipped than the Democrats to cope with the major problem before the country.

The number of respondents who shifted from Democratic to Republican between 1956 and 1960 who turned up in Dr. Gallup's samples is so small that one must be extremely wary of the data. Nevertheless, among those who voted in 1960, persons who had supported Stevenson but refused to vote for Kennedy must have numbered in the millions; and the suspicion grows that if one could get a reliable reading of the characteristics and motivations of the D-R voters, it would go far toward illuminating the special features of the 1960 election. Even the inadequate data that are available make it appear that the voters who switched Republican between 1956 and 1960 were a very special group.

Further light is shed on the peculiarities of the D-R's by looking at how they voted for other offices below the presidency. If many of these voters held issue positions at variance with orthodox Republican doctrine, they also might be expected to be less likely to support a Republican at the congressional level. This supposition is confirmed by the data in Table 5.10. Democratic and Republican standpatters were inclined in high degree to support a House nominee of the same party as their presidential choice, although there was slightly less party regularity among the R-R's than among the D-D's. New voters who were drawn to the respective party banners were also overwhelmingly likely to vote a straight ticket for president and House member. Again the number of respondents who switched from Democratic to Republican is small. Even so, the data create a strong suspicion that the D-R's differed markedly from the R-D's in the enthusiasm they had for the party whose presidential nominee they

TABLE 5.10. Patterns of presidential voting, 1956–1960, in relation to response to question: "For the U.S. House of Representatives, did you vote for the Republican candidate or for the Democratic candidate?"[a]

Congressional vote	D-D	R-D	0-D	0-R	D-R	R-R
Republican	3%	9%	9%	83%	51%	87%
Democratic	95	83	87	11	42	10
Other and No answer	2	8	4	6	7	3
	100	100	100	100	100	100
N	(612)	(321)	(154)	(147)	(84)	(840)

[a] AIPO 638-K, 11-15-60.

supported. Voters who switched Democratic between 1956 and 1960 tended to vote a straight ticket for president and House somewhat less than the Democratic stand-patters; but nonetheless an overwhelming majority of these voters did so. Among the D-R's, by contrast, the number whose party regularity in their voting carried over into the congressional contest was not much more than half.

A roughly similar pattern emerges when the frequency with which 1960 voters indulged in split-ticket voting at the state and local level as well as the national level is examined. All categories of Republican presidential voters were more likely to split their ticket than those who supported Kennedy in 1960. But only a quarter of the R-D's reported a split-ticket vote, compared with two thirds of the D-R's. The details of these relationships appear in Table 5.11.

Other characteristics of the 1960 D-R voters also command attention. They were more likely than any other group in our standard categories to have thought of voting for the presidential nominee of the opposite party at some point during the campaign. (Table 5.12.) They were also

TABLE 5.11. Patterns of presidential voting, 1956–1960, in relation to response to question: "For the various political offices, did you vote for all the candidates of one party—that is, a straight ticket—or did you vote for the candidates of different parties?"[a]

Response	D-D	R-D	0-D	0-R	D-R	R-R
Straight ticket	79%	70%	75%	46%	29%	61%
Split ticket	20	26	24	50	64	37
Don't know and No answer	1	4	1	4	7	2
	100	100	100	100	100	100
N	(612)	(321)	(154)	(147)	(84)	(840)

[a] AIPO 638-K, 11-15-60.

136

TABLE 5.12. Patterns of presidential voting, 1956–1960, in relation to response to question: "At any time did you intend to vote for the other candidate—that is (Kennedy) (Nixon)?"[a]

Response	D-D	R-D	0-D	0-R	D-R	R-R
Yes	5%	18%	20%	16%	30%	8%
No	92	79	79	84	65	91
No answer	3	3	1	—	5	1
	100	100	100	100	100	100
N	(612)	(321)	(154)	(147)	(84)	(840)

[a] AIPO 638-K, 11-15-60.

more likely to have made up their mind in the final week of the campaign. (Table 5.13.) And, in overwhelming degree, they were of the Protestant religious faith.

It is well to remember that voters who were D-R's in 1960 were voters who said they had supported the Democratic presidential nominee in 1956, despite a Republican landslide that year in the presidential race. Yet four years later, when nation-wide the Democratic party's fortunes were sharply improved, these voters were unable to vote for the Democratic presidential nominee. The data suggest—though because of the small number of cases they do not prove—that these voters showed far less enthusiasm on issues for the G.O.P. than any other of our groups of voters who supported the Republican party. They also were more likely to vote Democratic for other offices, and, apparently, to waver before they cast their lot with Richard Nixon. How many of these voters were casting a vote against Kennedy on the grounds of his religion, the data at hand do not permit us to say. It is a good guess, however, that the number of such voters among the D-R's was large.

Throughout the 1960 campaign Democratic strategists were plagued by the question of what sort of position their candidate should take publicly concerning the Eisen-

TABLE 5.13. Patterns of presidential voting, 1956–1960, in relation to response to question: "When did you make up your mind definitely to vote for (Kennedy) (Nixon)?"[a]

Response	D-D	R-D	0-D	0-R	D-R	R-R
Have always voted Democratic or Republican	11%	9%	13%	3%	2%	3%
Some time before the convention	7	8	4	9	1	5
At time of convention[b]	50	41	25	58	53	65
During the TV debates	13	18	25	8	14	10
Few weeks or a month before election[c]	7	9	7	10	4	7
A day to a week before election	8	8	20	10	25	5
No answer, Don't know, Other	4	7	6	2	1	5
	100	100	100	100	100	100
N	(612)	(321)	(154)	(147)	(84)	(840)

[a] AIPO 638-K, 11-15-60.
[b] When he got the nomination for president; at the convention; when he was chosen as a candidate; at the very beginning of the campaign; early this summer.
[c] With no mention of the TV debates.

hower Administration. The data in Table 5.14 show why. Among those who had an opinion, the American public tended to approve of Eisenhower's performance as president by a margin of roughly two to one. The figures underscore another major difference between the elections of 1960 and 1952 in the strategic situation confronting the two parties and in the clustering of attitudes with relevance for the vote. In 1952 the incumbent Democratic Administration headed by President Truman was unpopular. Of those with an opinion one way or another, less than 40 per cent approved of Truman's performance as president (Table 4.4). Attacks on the Administration, and

TABLE 5.14. Switching in presidential voting preference, 1956–1960, in relation to response to question: "Do you approve or disapprove of the way Eisenhower is handling his job as President?"[a]

Response	% of 1956 D's, D-R	% of 1956 R's, R-D	% of new voters, D
Approve	22 (685)	20 (3,221)	43 (1,292)
Disapprove	4 (1,281)	60 (535)	81 (655)
No opinion	13 (242)	59 (201)	79 (351)

[a] A consolidation of AIPO 635-K, 9-7-60; 636-K, 9-26-60; 637-K, 10-18-60. Total N for the combined samples, 9,515.

attempts to link Stevenson with Truman promised a political payoff, and attack the Republicans did. But in 1960 Eisenhower's popularity remained high; and Nixon, unlike Stevenson in 1952, sought assiduously to identify himself with the incumbent Administration of his party. At a meeting of Kennedy and his closest advisers at Hyannisport on October 1, 1960, the Democrats discussed their own counterstrategy. They decided, Theodore White reports, that Kennedy must not attack Eisenhower but only ignore him.[19]

The data in Table 5.14 highlight the way the 1960 results featured a net shift of voters sufficient to elect Kennedy superimposed on a basic distribution of attitudes weighted heavily in favor of President Eisenhower. Kennedy, of course, did very well among those who disapproved of Eisenhower. Of 1956 Eisenhower voters who in 1960 disapproved of the President, six in ten shifted to Kennedy. But the votes of those who disapproved of the General alone would have fallen far short of a majority. Kennedy also made large net gains among those who had no opinion concerning the Eisenhower record as

19. White, Making of President 1960, p. 321.

president, and on balance he also gained strength among those who approved of Eisenhower's performance.[20]

There was a very sharp divergence between the stand-patters of the two parties in the way they appraised the Eisenhower record. (Table 5.15.) Republican standpatters, of course, were strongly favorable. Yet even the kindly image of General Eisenhower was unable to prevent a sizable majority of the D-D's from holding persis-

TABLE 5.15. Patterns of presidential voting preference, 1956–1960, in relation to response to question: "Do you approve or disapprove of the way Eisenhower is handling his job as President?"[a]

Response	D-D	R-D	0-D	0-R	D-R	R-R
Approve	27%	59%	41%	78%	64%	89%
Disapprove	62	30	39	13	21	7
No opinion	10	11	20	8	13	3
No answer	1	b	b	1	2	1
	100	100	100	100	100	100
N	(1,990)	(1,088)	(1,362)	(944)	(236)	(2,889)

[a] A combination of AIPO 635-K, 9-7-60; 636-K, 9-26-60, and 10-18-60, 637-K.

[b] Less than one half of 1 per cent.

tent doubts about his capacities as president. But in their attitude toward Eisenhower the R-D's, a group so essential to Kennedy's success, were much more charitable than the D-D's. Although the R-D's intended to vote for Kennedy, they approved of Eisenhower's performance by two to one. From the Democrats' standpoint, the decision

20. The proportion of 1956 Democratic voters who liked Eisenhower who switched Republican and the proportion of 1956 Republican voters who approved of Eisenhower who switched Democratic were close to the same. But many more voters who approved of Eisenhower had voted Republican in 1956 than had voted Democratic. Hence in absolute terms Kennedy gained strength among those favorably disposed toward Eisenhower.

TABLE 5.16. Patterns of presidential voting preference, 1956–1960, in relation to response to question: "Generally speaking, how much interest would you say you have in politics—a great deal, a fair amount, only a little, or no interest at all?"[a]

Level of interest	D-D	R-D	0-D	0-R	D-R	R-R
Great deal	32%	19%	16%	14%	30%	30%
Fair amount	46	59	41	44	55	53
Only a little	20	20	34	35	14	16
None at all	2	2	9	7	1	1
	100	100	100	100	100	100
N	(1,440)	(756)	(965)	(667)	(151)	(1,946)

[a] A consolidation of AIPO 636-K, 9-26-60, and 637-K, 10-18-60. Total N for the combined sample, 6,608.

to muffle their attacks on Eisenhower may well have been a wise one.

The data on the 1960 election enable us to supplement and elaborate the discussion initiated in the preceding chapter of the outlooks and characteristics of our categories of voters, with special reference to the oddities of the switchers.* The inspection of the same phenomenon in a series of elections may require a modification of the findings that might be drawn from the inspection of a single election.

Level of interest, as measured by the voter's own appraisal, it was shown in Table 4.14, differed among standpatters, switchers, and new voters in 1952. Somewhat more marked contrasts prevailed in level of interest among these categories of persons in 1960, as may be seen from Table 5.16. Moreover, a clearer relationship prevailed between level of interest and disposition to switch in 1960 than had been the case in 1952. The proportions, by level

* Editor's note: With this sentence the narrative by V. O. Key, Jr., begins again.

of interest, reporting an intention to switch (either R-D or D-R) in 1960 from their 1956 vote were as follows:

Great deal of interest	Fair amount	Little	None
15%	24%	22%	33%
(1,229)	(2,243)	(764)	(57)*

These variations in switching rates were most marked among 1956 Republican voters, whose reported switching intentions, by level of interest, were:

Great deal of interest	Fair amount	Little	None
20%	30%	32%	51%
(726)	(1,490)	(453)	(33)†

The data certainly suggest that disposition to switch voting preference from 1956 to 1960 tended to increase with a decline in self-rated level of interest in politics. Yet this variation arose chiefly from among those shifting from a Republican to a Democratic vote. The rates of shifting from Stevenson in 1956 to Nixon in 1960 differed scarcely at all with level of interest.[21]

When the data of Tables 4.14 and 5.16 are compared we may be able better to place the phenomenon of the behavior of the low-interest and high-interest voter. In both 1952 and 1960 the standpatters, both R-R and D-D, had relatively high average levels of interest. In both instances, too, the switchers to the prevailing side, the D-R's in 1952 and the R-D's in 1960, showed a somewhat

* Editor's note: These figures cited by Key are based on the data from AIPO 637-K, 10-18-60.

† Editor's note: These figures cited by Key, like the data in Table 5.16, are based on a consolidation of AIPO 636-K, 9-26-60, and 637-K, 10-18-60.

21. The D-R rates for the interest levels in the order listed in the text were: 9%, 11%, 7%, 8%.

lower average level of interest than the standpatters. On
the other hand, the switchers who moved counter to the
prevailing trend, the R-D's in 1952 and the D-R's in
1960, had as high an average level of interest as did the
standpatters whom they joined. Some genuine concern
evidently was required to move against the tide. In both
instances the extremely low levels of interest were to be
found among the nonvoters of the preceding election—
those too young then to vote, insufficiently interested,
or otherwise moved to inaction.*

Another approach to the question whether switchers
are less informed and perhaps less involved than standpatters is to ascertain the relative frequency with which
different types of voters gave "don't know" or "no
opinion" answers to policy questions. In 1952, it will be
recalled, the switchers seemed to include no more persons with "no opinion" than did the standpatters of both
parties on two policy questions for which data were available. In 1960, however, on the question of which party
would do the "best job of keeping the country prosperous," the switchers were more likely to have no opinion
than were the standpatters. (Table 5.7.) On the question
of which party would do the best job of handling the
most important problem facing the country, the switchers
also had slightly more no opinions or no answers than the
standpatters. (Table 5.9.) On the question whether they
approved of Eisenhower's performance as president, there
were also more no opinions among those who switched
Republican than among the Republican standpat group.
Voters who shifted Democratic between 1956 and 1960,
however, were no more likely to lack an opinion on Eisenhower's performance than were Democratic standpatters.
(Table 5.15.) On all three questions, new voters were

* Editor's note: Narrative by V. O. Key, Jr., stops here again.

143

more likely to have no opinion than were the standpatters of the party to whose support they moved. Although the precise figures varied from question to question, therefore, both switching voters and new voters appeared to be less likely to hold opinions on these policy questions than were the standpat voters in 1960.

Other differences among the various categories of voters were in evidence in 1960. Both the 1960 switchers and new voters were less likely to feel very strongly about their choice in the presidential contest than were the standpatters. (Table 5.17.) On the other hand, in their average level of education, neither the switchers or the new voters differed significantly from the standpatters in 1960, a finding that suggests the importance of looking for differences among new voters, switchers, and standpatters in terms of their motivations and attitudes rather than in terms of their objective social characteristics in 1960. (Table 5.18.)

Another way to look at the qualities of switching voters and new voters is to examine the frequency with which

TABLE 5.17. Patterns of presidential voting preference, 1956–1960, in relation to response to question: "Right now, how strongly do you feel about your choice—very strongly, fairly strongly, or not strongly at all?"[a]

Response	D-D	R-D	0-D	0-R	D-R	R-R
Very strongly	66%	46%	49%	46%	36%	69%
Fairly strongly	27	39	37	42	43	23
Not strongly at all	7	14	12	10	20	8
Don't know	[b]	1	2	2	1	[b]
	100	100	100	100	100	100
N	(1,987)	(1,084)	(1,353)	(934)	(192)	(2,808)

[a] A consolidation of AIPO 635-K, 9-7-60; 636-K, 9-26-60; and 637-K, 10-18-60. Total N for the combined sample, 9,515.

[b] Less than one half of 1 per cent.

TABLE 5.18. Patterns of presidential voting, 1956–1960, in relation to level of education[a]

Education	D-D	R-D	O-D	O-R	D-R	R-R
Grade school	41%	33%	43%	20%	8%	24%
High school	40	54	34	48	50	44
College	16	9	16	24	37	26
Trade school	3	4	6	5	5	6
No answer	—	—	1	3	—	—
	100	100	100	100	100	100
N	(612)	(321)	(154)	(147)	(84)	(840)

[a] AIPO 638-K, 11-15-60.

they vote. In 1960 the Gallup poll interviewers asked this question: "How often would you say you vote—always, nearly always, part of the time, or seldom?" Undoubtedly the answers to this question were not a perfect measure of the frequency with which the respondents actually voted. Probably some citizens were unable to resist the temptation to overstate the faithfulness with which they performed this act of civic virtue. Yet the responses provide a useful, though rough, indication of the frequency with which various groups of respondents voted, and the findings that emerge from Table 5.19 are of some interest.

Voters who switched with the prevailing tide (R-D) were somewhat less likely than Democratic standpatters to report that they "always" voted. They were a little more likely than the standpatters to acknowledge that they voted only "part of the time." The difference in the frequency with which the two groups of voters reported going to the polls, however, was not great. And the D-R's, those who were switching against the dominant electoral tide, were apparently almost as frequent voters as the Republican standpatters whom they joined. Here again

TABLE 5.19. Patterns of presidential voting preference, 1956–1960, in relation to response to question: "How often would you say you vote—always, nearly always, part of the time, or seldom?"[a]

Voting frequency	D-D	R-D	0-D	0-R	D-R	R-R
Always	74%	62%	21%	7%	66%	68%
Nearly always	21	28	12	12	28	25
Part of the time	4	9	19	17	6	6
Seldom	1	1	15	21	—	1
Other	b	b	7	10	—	b
Never	b	—	26	23	—	—
	100	100	100	100	100	100
N	(1,413)	(756)	(946)	(657)	(151)	(1,928)

[a] A consolidation of AIPO 636-K, 9-26-60, and 637-K, 10-18-60. Total N for combination, 6,608.

[b] Less than one half of 1 per cent.

it was the new voters who reported the really low rates of voting participation.

The view, first expressed in Chapter 4, that new voters as a group potentially contain numerous contributors to change, to flexibility, and to adjustment in the political system, finds added reinforcement in this examination of the 1960 election results. Their endorsement, on policy questions, of the party whose presidential nominee they support is less wholehearted than that of the party stand-patters whom they join. Both in 1952 and in 1960 they had the lowest levels of interest in politics. And, in 1960, they did not feel as strongly about their presidential choice as did the standpatters—although as a group they were about equal with the switchers on that score.

These differences between the new voters and the standpatters of both parties in 1960 make it tempting to imagine an election in which new voters—relatively less interested, relatively less involved, relatively less likely to vote—are mobilized overwhelmingly for one party and thus provide for it the key to victory. Perhaps in some electoral contest the new voters could play such a role, despite their relatively low voting participation in presidential elections. In 1960, however, the facts seem to be that the new voters split about evenly between Kennedy and Nixon. Kennedy did better among new voters in 1960 than Stevenson had done in 1956. But in order to win, Kennedy had to record large gains among voters who voted far more regularly and were substantially more interested in politics than the new voters of 1960.

The motivation and involvement in politics of new voters was lower than that of persons who had voted in the previous presidential contest both in 1952 and in 1960. But our comparative analysis of the two elections also indicates that the switchers of 1960 differed somewhat from the switchers of 1952. In 1952 the relationship between lower levels of interest in politics and a tendency to switch was relatively slight. In 1960 it was stronger. In 1952 switchers were no more likely to lack an opinion on policy questions than standpatters; in 1960 the frequency of "no opinion" responses among switchers was greater than among standpatters. Perhaps in an election where underlying group identifications are particularly salient and when no overriding policy concerns arise, the quality of the switching voters—in terms of their knowledge and interest in questions of public policy—will be lower.

Yet the main moral to be drawn from the findings seems to be that the characteristics of the switching voters can vary from election to election in response to the changing political topography of different election contests. The voters who are moved to switch in an election when the contrast between the candidates' public policy stands is sharply drawn may differ markedly from the voters who

147

switch when the distance separating the opposing candidates on issues is relatively narrow. And still another electoral situation may arise when the differences offered on policy are not large, but when some special characteristic of one of the candidates, such as his religion, becomes of major concern to large numbers of voters.

In 1960, with the election of the first Roman Catholic President in American history, group loyalties and antagonisms with a lengthy past loomed relatively larger as determinants of the vote than in some previous elections. Even then, however, many standpat voters in both party camps and many of the Democrats who returned to the Democratic party after having supported Eisenhower in 1956 had policy attitudes that were broadly consistent with their choice of a 1960 presidential nominee. Moreover, this predominance of considerations of party, religion, and other group identifications in the 1960 voting was probably made possible in part precisely because the gap between the two candidates on major questions of public policy was not large. Group identification is a major factor to be used in accounting for the vote in 1960. But the odds are that the relative importance and the strength of the relationships between switching and policy preferences would have been considerably greater if Barry Goldwater, not Richard Nixon, had been the Republican presidential nominee in 1960.

CONCLUSIONS

(Editor's note: The following is a transcript of V. O. Key, Jr.'s hand-written notes for the final chapter he planned to write. Slight changes have been made in punctuation, and three words have been inserted in brackets.)

Last chapter

For conclusions—

SHIFTING—

Of the supporters [of the "ins"]:

> Those at odds with policy of "ins" are most likely to defect—at times extremely high correlations.
> Those in agreement with position most likely to stand steadfast.

Of the supporters of the outs:

> Those who find its policies most congenial are most likely to remain loyal.
> Those who have come to concur with the ins are most likely to defect.

Of those with no opinion:

> A mid position between the policy supporters and

149

dissidents. (Person with no view on one issue, though, may dissent on another.)

In comment on general findings, final chapter—

Probably confirms the significance of Angus Campbell's model built on party identification. Standpatters stay by the party even though they agree with the opposition party. But those who agree with their party are most inclined to stay with it. Policy preference reinforces party loyalty. Those whose policy preference conflicts with their party voting record are most likely to defect.

All these patterns of behavior are consistent with the supposition that voters, or at least a large number of them, are moved by their perceptions and appraisals of policy and performance. They like or don't like the performance of government.

Several objections may be raised to the attribution of significance to the parallelism of policy preference and the direction of the vote. The busy citizen may simply make things look tidy by light-heartedly responding to policy questions in a manner that makes him look like a consistent fellow. Doubtless this occurs to some unknown extent; yet its import is to be discounted, for a voter must have a fair amount of information to simulate a consistent pattern of preferences. A more weighty objection is that policy preferences may not be expressions of an independent belief but merely views that persons identified with a political party perceive as the orthodox party line. This acceptance of the party line, it has been shown by Angus Campbell, occurs most markedly among persons with a strong party identification. Cues of party leadership certainly shape the policy preferences of many persons, but the significance of that phenomenon for our broad argument is another matter. This type of formation of policy attitudes must be limited in the main to two of our categories: the standpatters of each party and the party identifiers among the nonvoters at the preceding election. The switchers, the D-R's and the R-D's who turn up in the millions at each election, evidently are not party stalwarts who rely on the leaders of their own party for their policy outlooks or their candidate preferences.

INDEX

Age, and voting volatility, 83n
Agricultural Adjustment Act, 32
AIPO, *see* American Institute of
    Public Opinion
American Farm Bureau, 88-89
American Federation of Labor
    (AFL), supports Truman, 49
American Institute of Public Opin-
    ion (Gallup poll), xiii, xxi, 12,
    21n, 70n; mentioned, 3, 13n,
    35, 47n, 49n, 72n, 90n, 95n,
    105n, 123, 129, 130n, 132, 142n,
    145, and in footnotes to the
    tables. *See also* Gallup, George

Bach, Beverly, xix
Benson, Ezra Taft, 88-89
Berelson, Bernard, 4n, 10n, 93, 94,
    101n
British: in Second World War, 50-
    51; Suez attack, 80
Brookings Institution, xviin
Bureau of Labor Statistics, 71n

Campbell, Angus, 4n, 10, 15n, 26n,
    29, 30n, 52n, 55n, 69n, 71n, 73n,
    75n, 83n, 89, 90n, 92n, 93, 110n,
    114n, 150
Castro, Fidel, 107, 130
Catholic voters, 116, 118-120, 123n
China, 64
Civil rights, 110
Class conflict, in 1930's, 33-34
Class polarization, 34-35, 67-69.
    See also Status polarization
Communism, 130
Congress of Industrial Organiza-

tions (CIO), supports Truman,
    49
Congress, U.S.: attempts to aid
    farmer, 32; conflicts with Eisen-
    hower, 109-110
Converse, Philip E., 4n, 15n, 26n,
    30n, 69n, 110n, 114n, 117n,
    118n
Cooper, Homer C., 55n
Correlations between voting and
    policy preferences, 59-60, also
    passim
Cuba, 107-108, 130
Cummings, Milton C., Jr., bio-
    graphical, xvii

Daudt, H., 18n
David, Paul T., 121n
Debates, on television, 112
Defense and preparedness, 130
Democrats, *passim* throughout book
Depression, 31
Dewey, Thomas E., 50, 57-59, 77;
    mentioned, 15n, 72, 103, 121
Dulles, John Foster, 80

Economic growth, issue in *1960*
    campaign, 109
Economic problems, 131
Education, 95-96, 110, 131
Eisenhower, Dwight D.: *1956* over-
    recall of vote for in *1952*, 13;
    and *1952* election, 66-67, 71-73,
    77-78, 92-93; achieves Korean
    settlement, 79; and *1956* elec-
    tion, 79, 80, 82, 87-90, 113; con-
    flicts with Democratic Congress,

153

INDEX

109-110; attitudes on civil rights and medical care, 110; mentioned, xii, 5, 10, 12, 16, 63, 74, 75, 84, 85, 100, 108, 109, 112, 117, 119, 123, 124, 126, 139, 140, 148

Eisenhower Administration, 86n, 137-138

Eldersveld, S. J., 18n

Election returns, compared to output of an echo chamber, 2-3

Elections: of 1932, 29, 34, 111; of 1936, 29, 33, 34, 41, 111-113; of 1938, 47n; of 1940, 10, 17n, 22-23, 29, 35-38, 42-51 passim, 77; of 1944, 17n, 22-23, 29, 35-36, 49, 67, 77, 102-103; of 1948, 17n, 22-23, 29, 35-36, 49-50, 67, 77; of 1952, 10, 63-78 passim, 92-93, 97-98, 111-113, 138-139; of 1954, 79; of 1956, 15, 23, 69, 79-90 passim; of 1960, xvii, 15, 22, 25, 26, 107-148 passim; of 1964, xiv-xv

Electoral behavior studies, 3-4

Electorate: as retrospective judge, xii, 61, 77; moved by concern about policy questions, 7-8; functions of in democratic process, 60-62; unreality of static conception of, 105n

Elmira study, 101n

England, in Second World War, 50-51; Suez attack, 80

Erie County, Ohio, study of 1940 campaign in, 10

Farm policy, 44-46, 87-88, 131

Father image, xi-xii

Federal aid to education, 110

Federal government, transformation of after 1932 Democratic victory, 31-33

Foreign policy, 50, 74, 130

French, Suez attack, 80

Gallup, George, 12, 57, 72, 84, 98, 125, 130, 134

Gallup poll, see American Institute of Public Opinion

Gaudet, Hazel, 4n, 10n

Goldwater, Barry M., xiv, xv, 148

Government regulation of business, as issue, 44-45

Governmental actions of 1930's, impact on voters, 33

Great Depression, 31

Group identifications, importance of in 1960, 113-114

Group imperatives, ix

Gurin, Gerald, 4n, 10n, 73n

Harding, Warren G., 121

Harris, Louis, 74n

Hartley, Eugene, 69n

Home Owners' Loan Corporation, 31-32

Hoover, Herbert, 121

Houston Ministerial Association, 118

Hungarian uprising, 80

"In-and-out" voters, 22

"Independent" voters, 92-93

"Ins," supporters of, vote related to policy preferences, 149

Israel, 80

Jews: reaction to Suez Canal policy and the vote in 1956, 86n; vote in 1960, 116, 118

Johns Hopkins University, xviin

Juvenile delinquency, 130n

Kelley, Stanley, Jr., 121

Kennedy, John F.: recall of presidential vote for in mid-November 1960, 13n; proportion of 1960 vote for received from standpatters, switchers, and new voters, 25; number of switchers to, compared with number of switchers to Nixon, 26; religion a major issue in campaign, 115, 118; runs behind most other Democratic candidates, 115; support for among new voters, 116-

154